Donna Kooler's
555 Fabulous
Cross-Stitch
Patterns

Donna Kooler's
555 Fabulous
Cross-Stitch
Patterns

Sterling Publishing Co., Inc. New York

A Sterling/Chapelle Book

For Kooler Design Studio, Inc.

Editor
Priscilla Timm

President
Donna Kooler

Executive Vice President
Linda Gillum

Vice President
Priscilla Timm

Creative Director
Deanna Hall West

Executive Assistant
Loretta Heden

Staff Designers
Barbara Baatz
Linda Gillum
Jorja Hernandez
Nancy Rossi
Sandy Orton

Contributing Artists
Donna Yuen
Pam Johnson
Holly DeFount

Design Assistants
Sara Angle
Anita Forfang
Laurie Grant
Virginia Hanley-Rivett
Marsha Hinkson
Arlis Johnson
Lori Patton
Char Randolph
Giana Shaw
Pam Whyte

For Chapelle Ltd.

Owner
Jo Packham

Editor
Leslie Ridenour

Staff
Joy Anckner
Malissa Boatwright
Kass Burchett
Rebecca Christensen
Amber Hansen
Shirley Heslop
Holly Hollingsworth
Susan Jorgensen
Susan Laws
Amanda McPeck
Barbara Milburn
Pat Pearson
Cindy Rooks
Cindy Stoeckl
Lorrie Young
Nancy Whitley

Photography
Kevin Dilley for Hazen Photography

Photography Styling
Susan Laws

Framer
Artist Touch, Ogden, UT

If you have any questions or comments or would like information on specialty products featured in this book, please contact:
Chapelle Ltd., Inc.
P.O. Box 9252
Ogden, UT 84409
(801) 621-2777
(801) 621-2788 (fax)

Library of Congress Cataloging-in-Publication Data

Kooler, Donna.
   Donna Kooler's 555 fabulous cross-stitch patterns.
      p.   cm.
   "A Sterling/Chapelle book."
   Includes index.
   ISBN 0-8069-3183-3
   1. Cross-stitch—Patterns.
   I. Title
TT778.C76K664   1996
746.44'3041—dc20   96-25869
                                    CIP

10 9 8 7 6 5 4 3

Published by Sterling Publishing Company, Inc.
387 Park Avenue South, New York, NY 10016
© 1996 by Chapelle Limited
Distributed in Canada by Sterling Publishing
c/o Canadian Manda Group, One Atlantic Avenue,
Suite 105, Toronto, Ontario, Canada M6K 3E7
Distributed in Great Britain and Europe by Cassell
PLC, Wellington House, 125 Strand,
London WC2R 0BB, England
Distributed in Australia by Capricorn Link
(Australia) Pty Ltd., P.O. Box 6651, Baulkham Hills,
Business Centre, NSW 2153, Australia
Printed and Bound in Hong Kong

Sterling ISBN 0-8069-3183-3

Contents

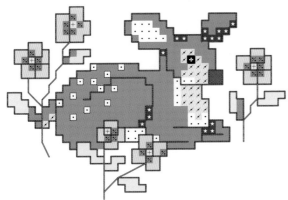
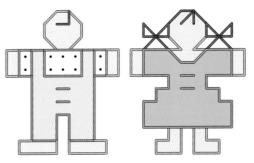
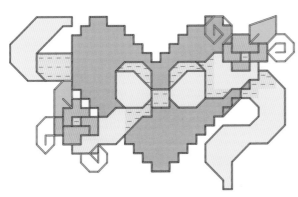
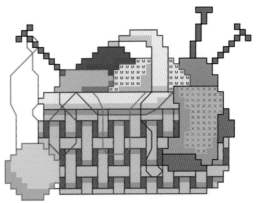
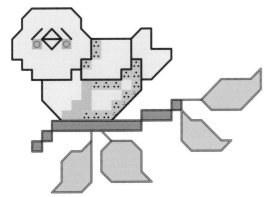

General Information

Introduction

Contained in this book are over 555 counted cross-stitch designs.

For each of the six chapters herein, we have stitched and photographed a sampler of several of the designs in the chapter. The individually graphed designs for these samplers have been placed on pages immediately following the photograph—usually the next four to six pages.

There is one color code for each sampler. This code falls on the last page of the individually graphed sampler designs.

The remaining designs in each chapter are not stitched nor photographed. Each page of graphed designs has its own color code.

To create one-of-a-kind motifs, vary colors in the graphed designs. The stitching possibilities will prove endless.

Fabric for Cross-stitch

Counted cross-stitch is usually worked on even-weave fabrics. These fabrics are manufactured specifically for counted-thread embroidery and are woven with the same number of vertical as horizontal threads per inch.

Because the number of threads in the fabric is equal in each direction, each stitch will be the same size. The number of threads per inch in even-weave fabrics

determines the size of a finished design.

Number of Strands

The number of strands used per stitch varies depending on the fabric used. Generally, the rule to follow for cross-stitching is three strands on Aida 11, two strands on Aida 14, one or two strands on Aida 18 (depending on desired thickness of stitches) and one strand on Hardanger 22.

For back-stitching, use one strand on all fabrics. When completing a french knot, use two strands and one wrap on all fabrics.

Preparing Fabric

Cut fabric at least 3" larger on all sides than finished design size to ensure enough space for desired assembly. If the design is used to embellish a project that will be finished further, check instructions for specific fabric allowances. A 3" margin is the minimum amount of space that allows for comfortably finishing the edges of the design.

To prevent fraying, whipstitch or machine-zigzag along raw edges or apply liquid fray preventer.

Needles for Cross-stitch

Needles should slip easily through fabric holes without piercing fabric threads. For fabric with 11 or fewer threads per inch, use a tapestry needle size 24; for 14 threads per inch, use a tapestry needle size 24 or 26; for 18 or more threads per inch, use a tapestry needle size 26.

Never leave needle in design area of fabric. It may leave rust or a permanent impression on fabric.

Floss

For each sampler and each page of graphed designs there is a color code. All numbers and color names on this code represent DMC brands of floss. Use 18" lengths of floss. For best coverage, separate strands. Dampen with wet sponge. Then put together number of strands required for fabric used.

Centering the Design

Fold the fabric in half horizontally, then vertically. Place a pin in the fold point to mark the center. Locate the center of the design on the graph. Begin stitching all designs at the center point of graph and fabric.

Securing the Floss

Insert needle up from the underside of the fabric at starting point. Hold 1" of thread behind the fabric and stitch over it, securing with the first few stitches. To finish thread, run under four or more stitches on the back of the design. Never knot floss, unless working on clothing.

Another method of securing floss is the waste knot. Knot floss and insert needle from the right side of the fabric about 1" from design area. Work several stitches over the thread to secure. Cut off the knot later.

General Information

Carrying Floss

To carry floss, weave floss under the previously worked stitches on the back. Do not carry thread across any fabric that is not or will not be stitched. Loose threads, especially dark ones, will show through the fabric.

Cleaning Completed Work

When stitching is complete, soak fabric in cold water with a mild soap for five to 10 minutes. Rinse well and roll in a towel to remove excess water. Do not wring. Place work face down on a dry towel and iron on warm setting until the fabric is dry.

Cross-stitch (X st)

Stitches are done in a row or, if necessary, one at a time in an area. Stitching is done by coming up through a hole between woven threads at A. Then, go down at B, the hole diagonally across from A. Come back up at C and down at D, etc. Complete the top stitches to create an "X". All top stitches should lie in the same direction. Come up at E and go down at B, come up at C and go down at F, etc.

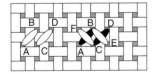

Backstitch (BS)

Pull the needle through at the point marked A. Then go down one opening to the right, at B. Then, come back up at C. Now,

go down one opening to the right, this time at "A".

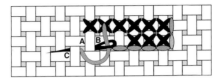

French Knot (FK)

Bring needle up at A, using two strands of embroidery floss. Loosely wrap floss once around needle. Place needle at B, next to A. Pull floss taut as you push needle down through fabric. Carry floss across back of work between knots.

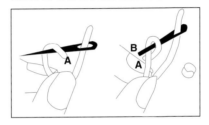

Long Stitch (LS)

Bring needle up at A; go down at B. Pull flat. Repeat A–B for each stitch. The length of the stitch should be the same as the length of the line on the design chart.

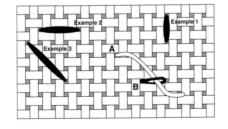

Lazy Daisy (LD)

Bring the needle up at A. Keep the thread flat, untwisted and full. Put the needle down through fabric at B and up through at C, keeping the thread under the needle to form a loop. Pull the thread through,

leaving the loop loose and full. To hold the loop in place, go down on other side of thread near C, forming a straight stitch over loop.

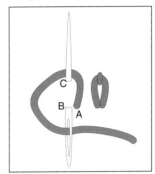

Couched Stitch (CS)

Complete a straight stitch the desired length of the design. Make sure floss is flat.

Make short tight straight stitches across base to "couch" the straight stitch (A–B). Come up on one side of the floss (C). Go down on the opposite side of the floss (D). Tack at varying intervals.

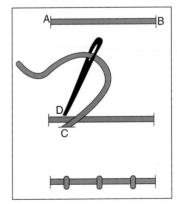

Flora
&
Fauna

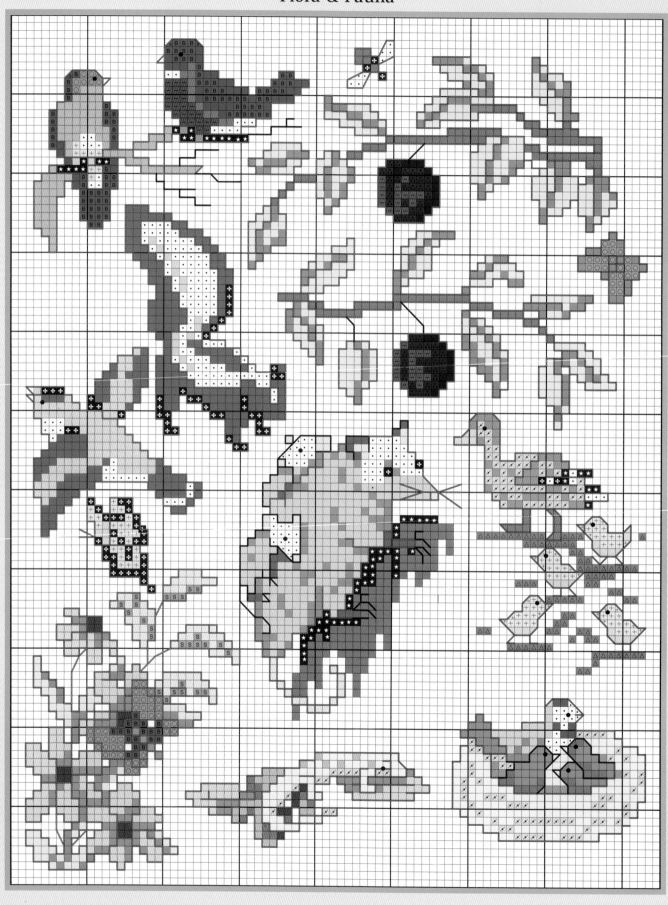

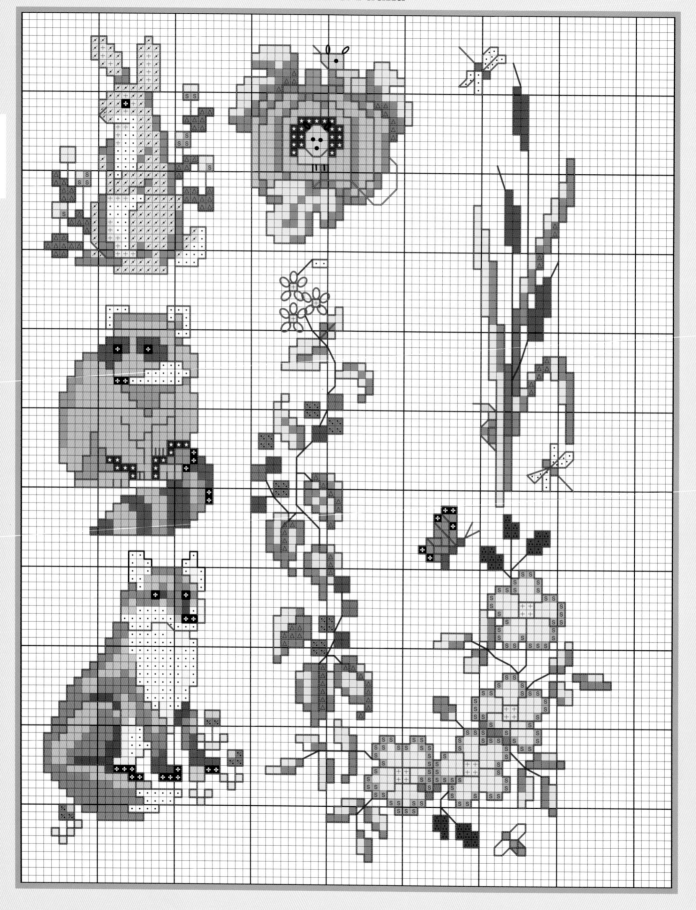

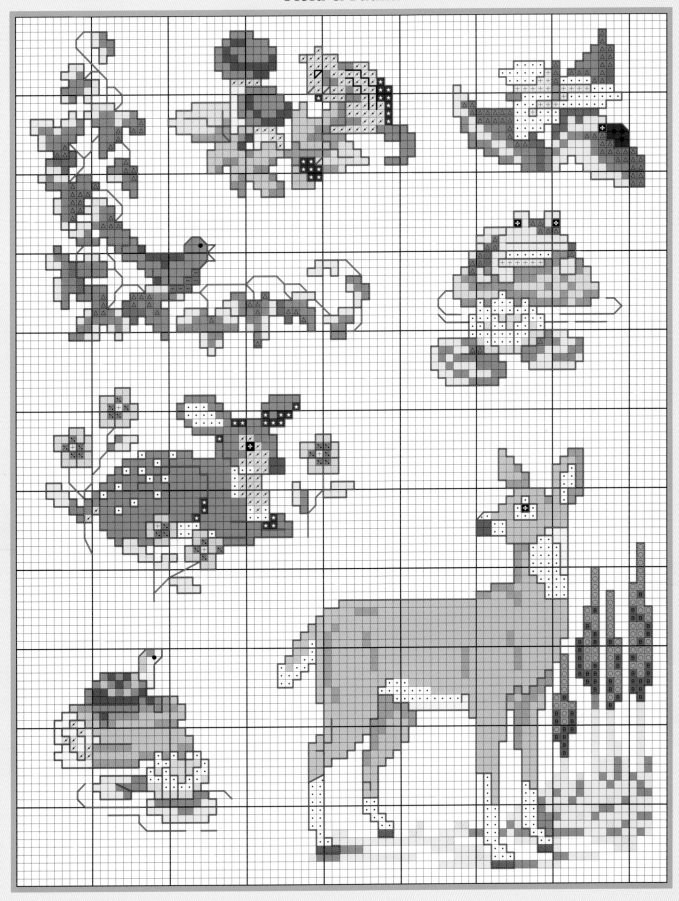

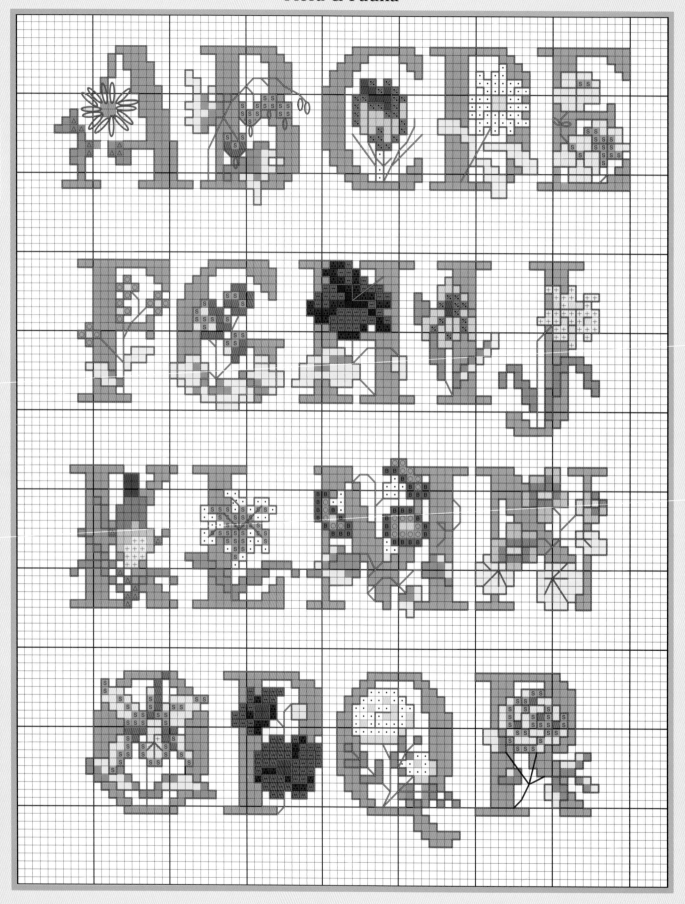

14

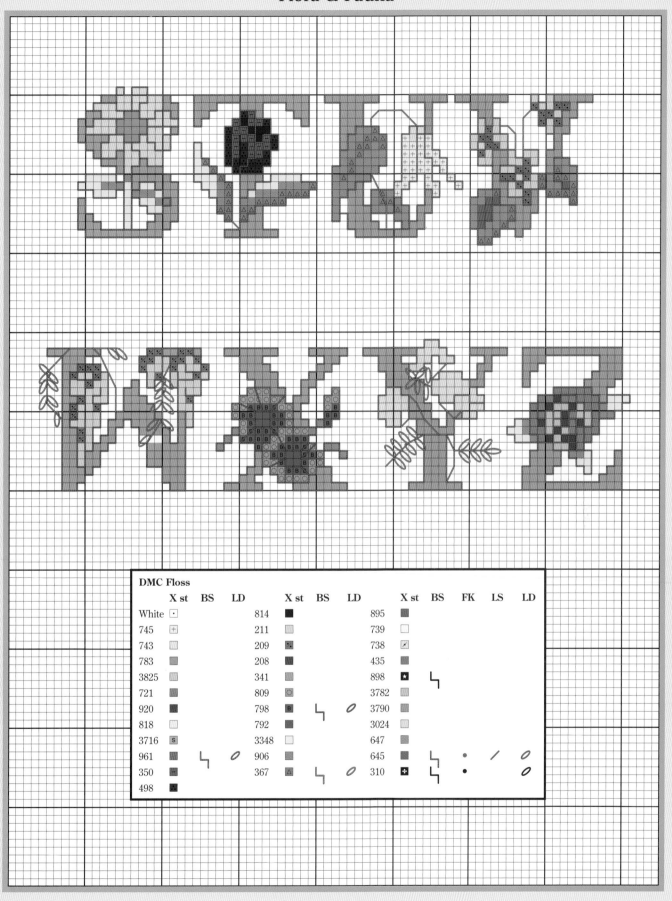

Flora & Fauna

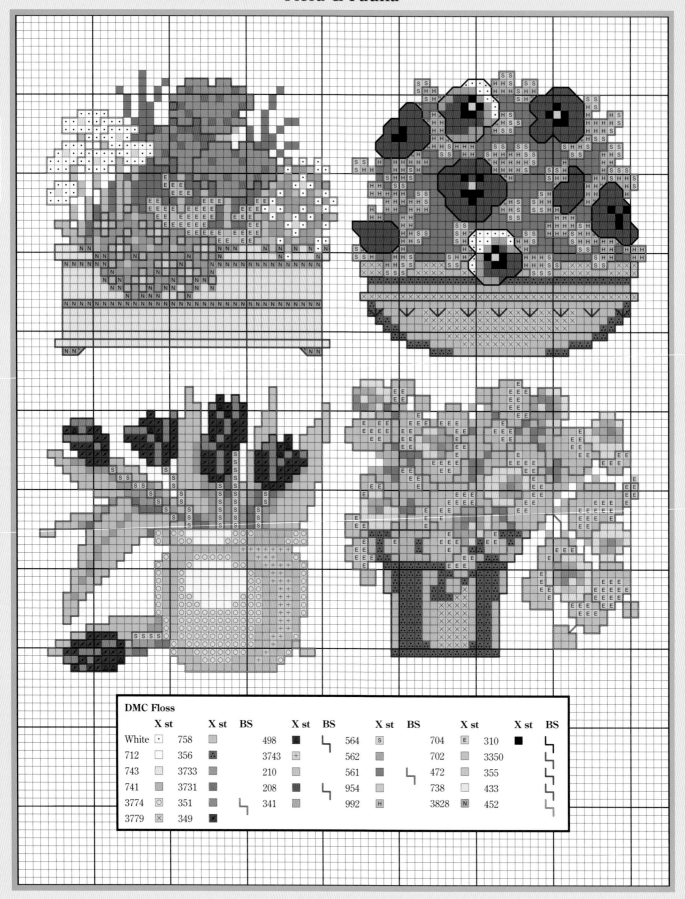

DMC Floss

	X st		X st	BS		X st	BS		X st	BS		X st	BS		X st		X st	BS
White	·	758			498			564	S		704	E	310				
712		356			3743	+		562			702		3350				
743		3733			210			561			472		355				
741		3731			208			954			738		433				
3774	○	351			341			992	H		3828		452	N			
3779	✕	349															

Flora & Fauna

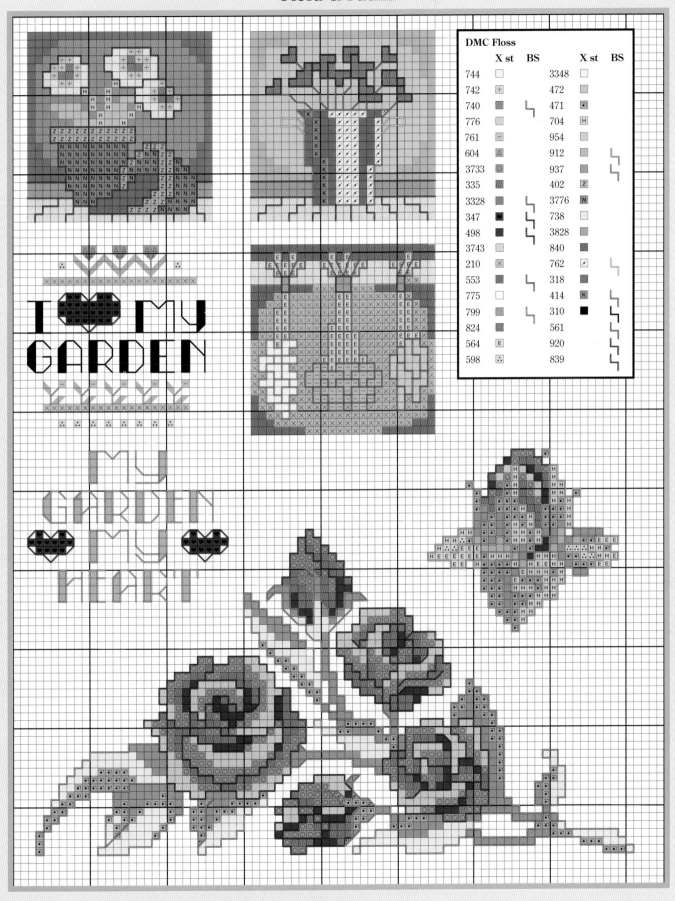

DMC Floss				
	X st	BS	X st	BS
744			3348	
742	+		472	
740		⌐	471	
776			704	H
761	−		954	
604	△		912	⌐
3733	⊙		937	
335			402	Z
3328		⌐	3776	N
347		⌐	738	
498		⌐	3828	
3743			840	
210	✕		762	⌐
553		⌐	318	
775		⌐	414	K ⌐
799		⌐	310	⌐
824			561	⌐
564	E		920	
598	∴		839	⌐

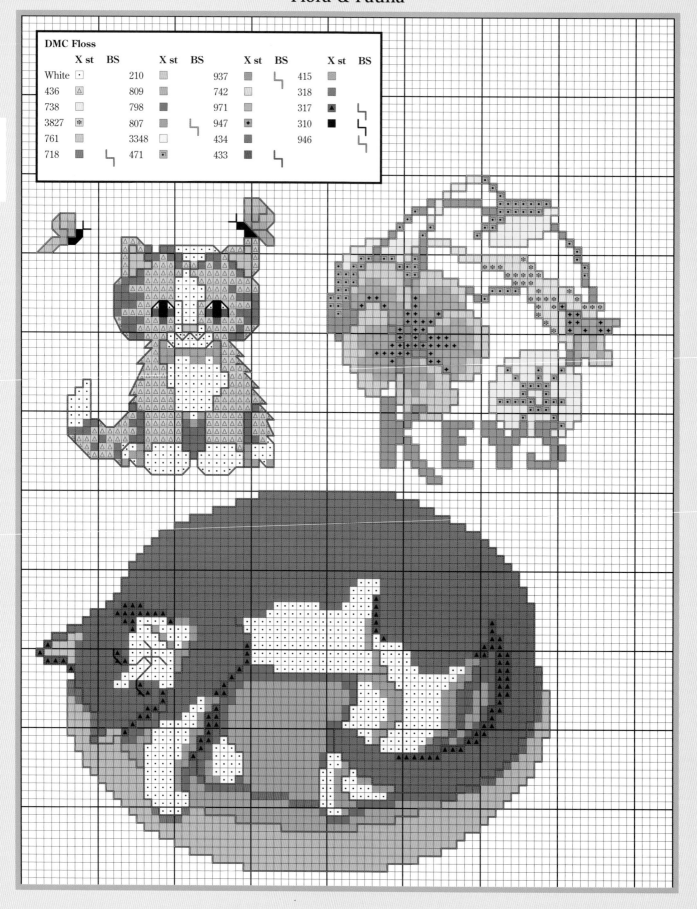

DMC Floss

	X st		X st		BS		X st	BS
White	·	920			844			
738		605			415			
743		760			317			
951	○	603			413			
758		964			310	■		
922		368			3328			
976		958			816			

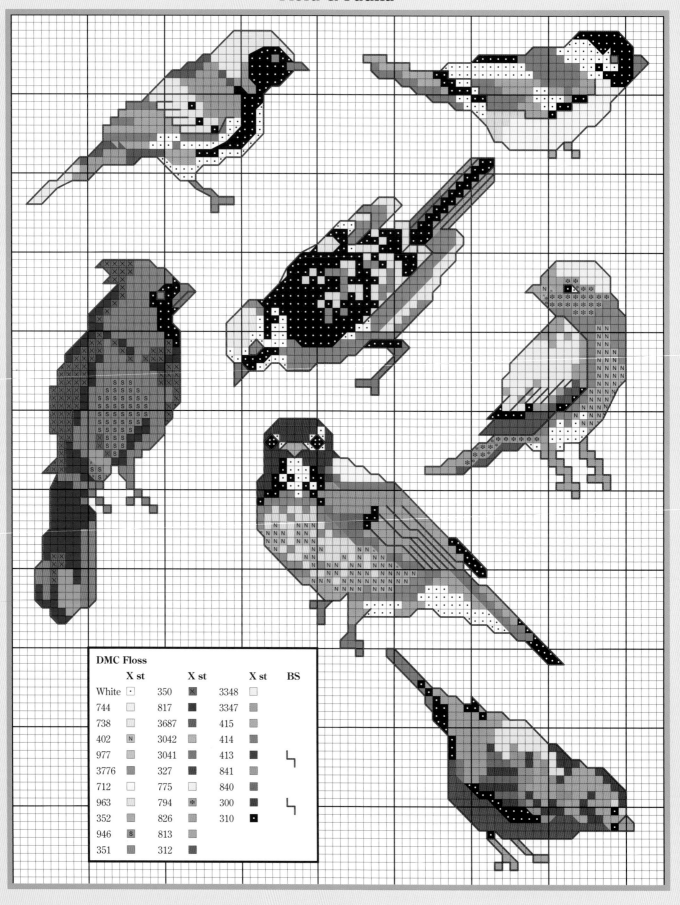

DMC Floss

	X st		X st		X st	BS
White	·	350		3348		
744		817		3347		
738		3687		415		
402	N	3042		414		
977		3041		413		
3776		327		841		⌐
712		775		840		
963		794	✳	300		⌐
352		826		310	·	
946	S	813				
351		312				

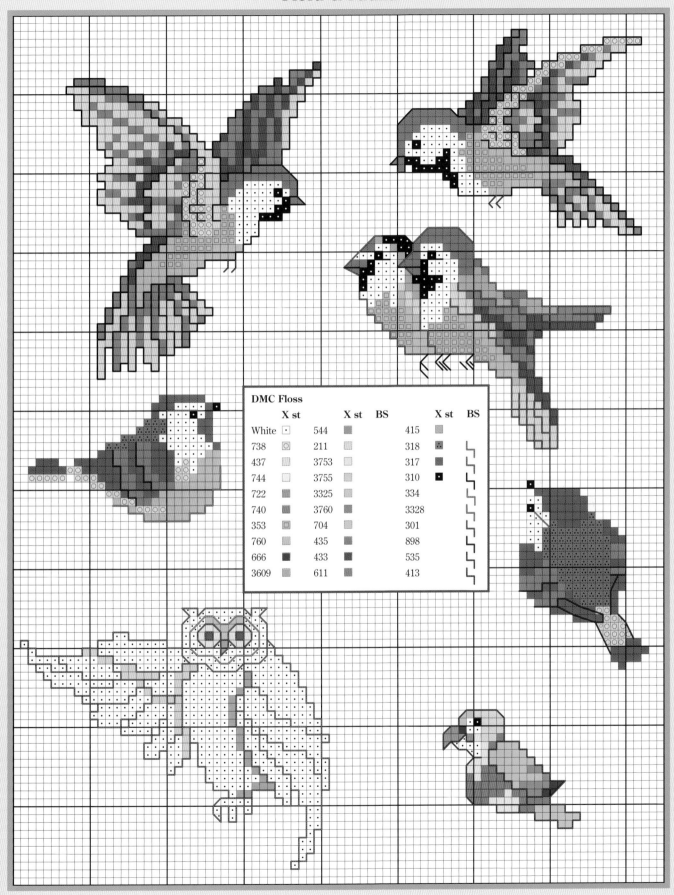

DMC Floss

	X st		X st	BS		X st	BS
White	·	544			415		
738		211			318		
437		3753			317		
744		3755			310		
722		3325			334		
740		3760			3328		
353		704			301		
760		435			898		
666		433			535		
3609		611			413		

Flora & Fauna

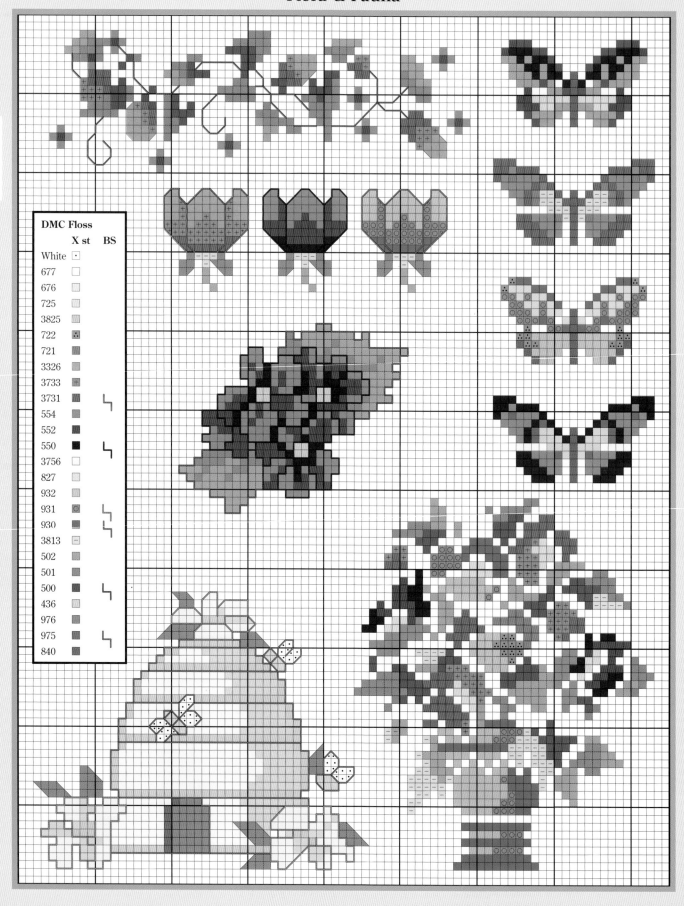

DMC Floss

	X st	BS
White	·	
677		
676		
725		
3825		
722		
721		
3326		
3733	+	
3731		⌐
554		
552		
550		⌐
3756		
827		
932		
931	◎	⌐
930		⌐
3813	−	
502		
501		
500		⌐
436		
976		
975		⌐
840		

Flora & Fauna

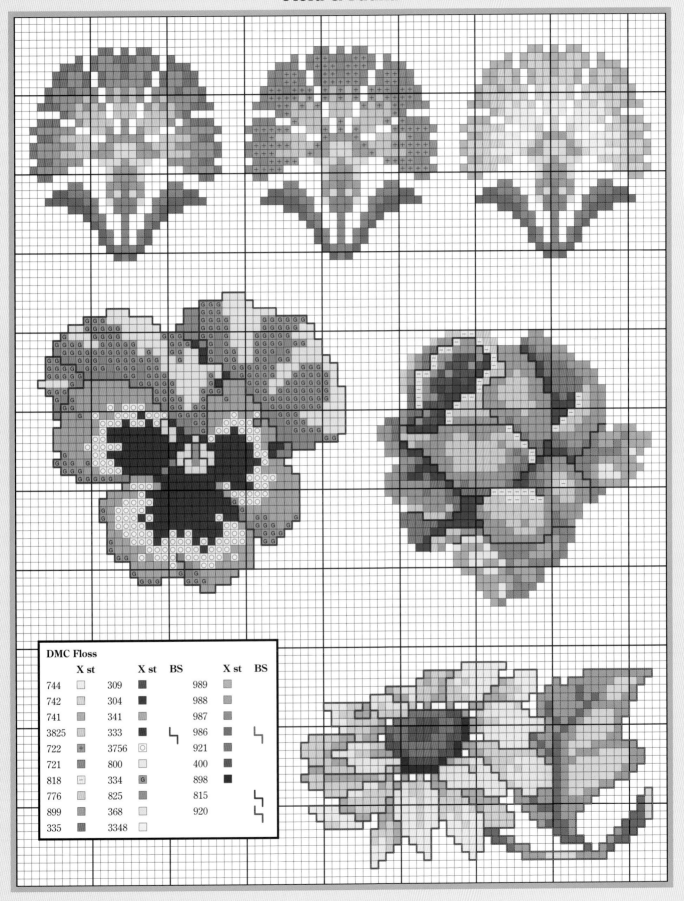

DMC Floss

	X st		X st	BS		X st	BS
744		309			989		
742		304			988		
741		341			987		
3825		333		⌐	986		⌐
722	+	3756	◎		921		
721		800			400		
818	–	334	G		898		
776		825			815		⌐
899		368			920		⌐
335		3348					

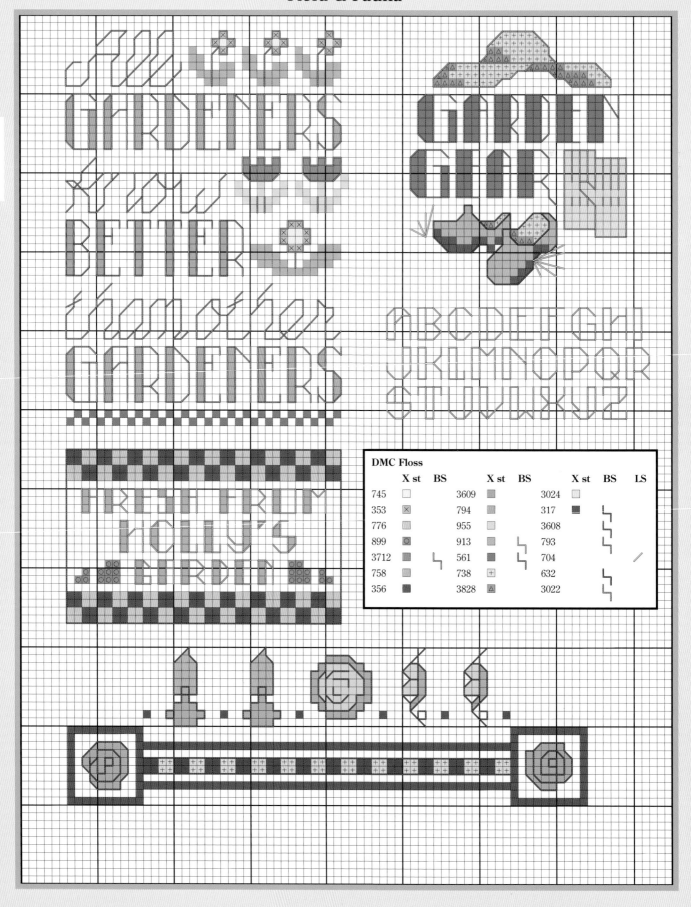

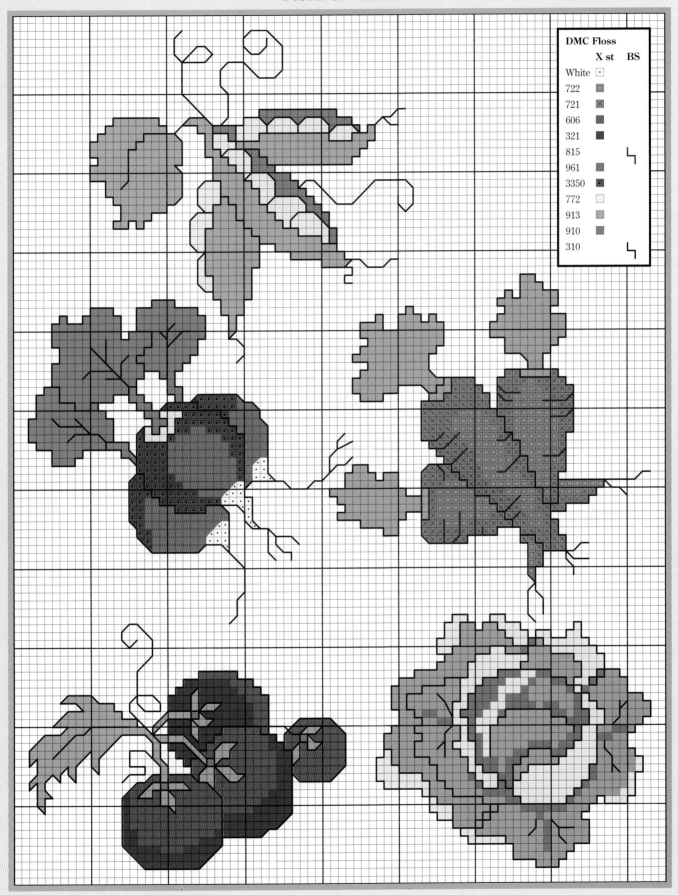

DMC Floss

	X st	BS
White	·	
722		
721	✕	
606		
321		
815		⌐
961		
3350		
772		
913		
910		
310		⌐

2
5

Friends
&
Family

Especially for You

Congratulations!

DAD.....

HAPPY BIRTHDAY

WORLD'S BEST!

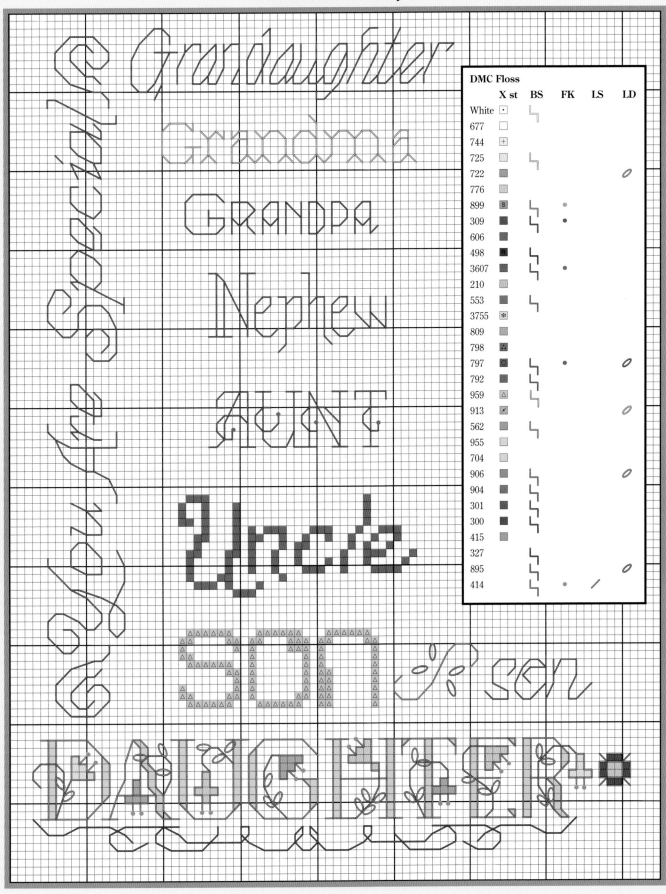

DMC Floss	X st	BS	FK	LS	LD
White	·	⌐			
677	☐				
744	+				
725		⌐			
722					⊘
776					
899	S	⌐	•		
309		⌐	•		
606					
498	R	⌐			
3607		⌐	•		
210					
553		⌐			
3755	✳				
809					
798	▦				
797	◎	⌐	•		⊘
792		⌐			
959	△				⊘
913	◿				⊘
562		⌐			
955					
704					
906		⌐			⊘
904		⌐			
301		⌐			
300		⌐			
415					
327		⌐			
895		⌐			⊘
414		⌐	•	/	

3
1

Friends & Family

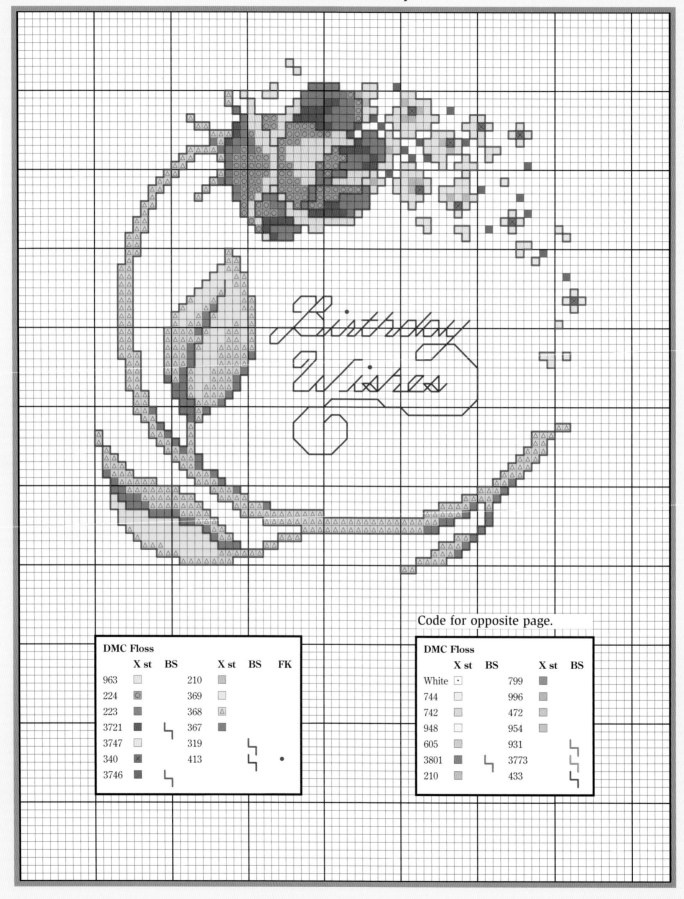

Code for opposite page.

DMC Floss

	X st	BS		X st	BS	FK
963			210			
224			369			
223			368			
3721		⌐	367			
3747			319			
340	✕		413		⌐	•
3746		⌐				

DMC Floss

	X st	BS		X st	BS
White	·		799		
744			996		
742			472		
948			954		
605			931		⌐
3801		⌐	3773		⌐
210			433		⌐

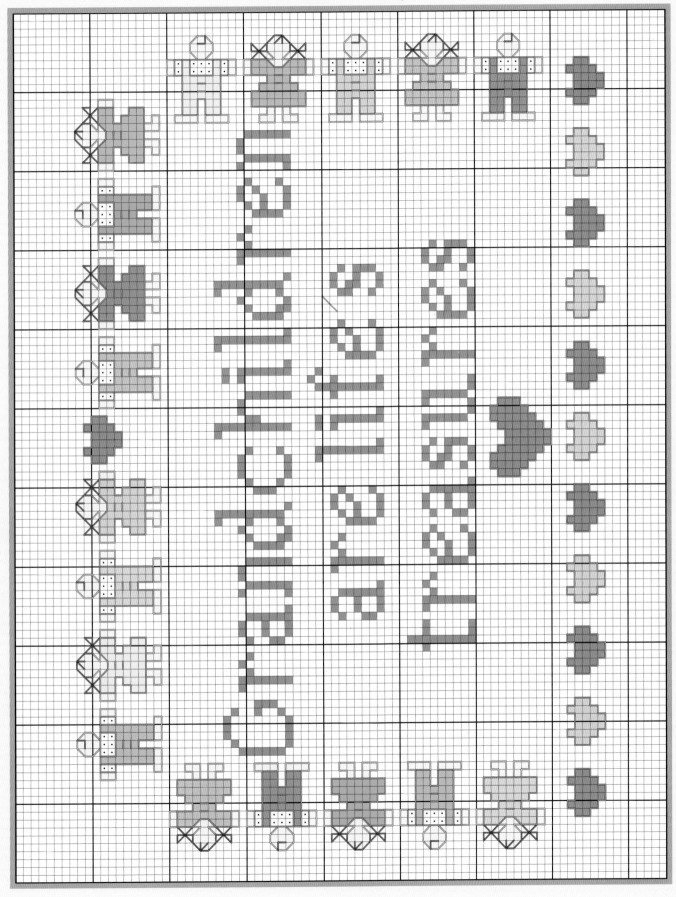

3
4

Mother

DMC Floss

	X st	BS		X st	BS
3078			498		⌐
3821			563		
3820	+	⌐	562		⌐
352			3787		⌐
666					

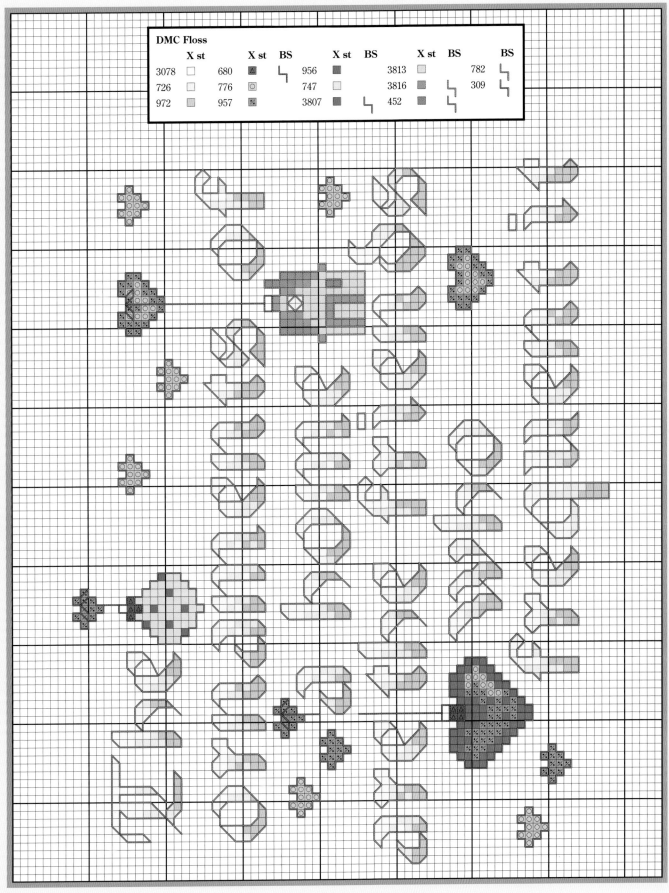

DMC Floss

X st		X st		BS	X st	BS	X st		BS		BS
3078	☐	680	▲	⌐	956	■	3813	☐		782	⌐
726	☐	776	◉		747	☐	3816	■	⌐	309	⌐
972	▨	957	▨		3807	■	⌐	452	■	⌐	

DMC Floss

	X st	BS		X st	BS	FK
White	·		3802	■	⌐	
712	☐		775	☐		
727	☐		800	⊡		
743	◎		738	⊞		
783	▨		402	▨		
963	▨		3776	▨		
224	▨		318	▨		
223	▨	⌐	780		⌐	
340	▨		400		⌐	
210	▨		413		⌐	•
355	■					

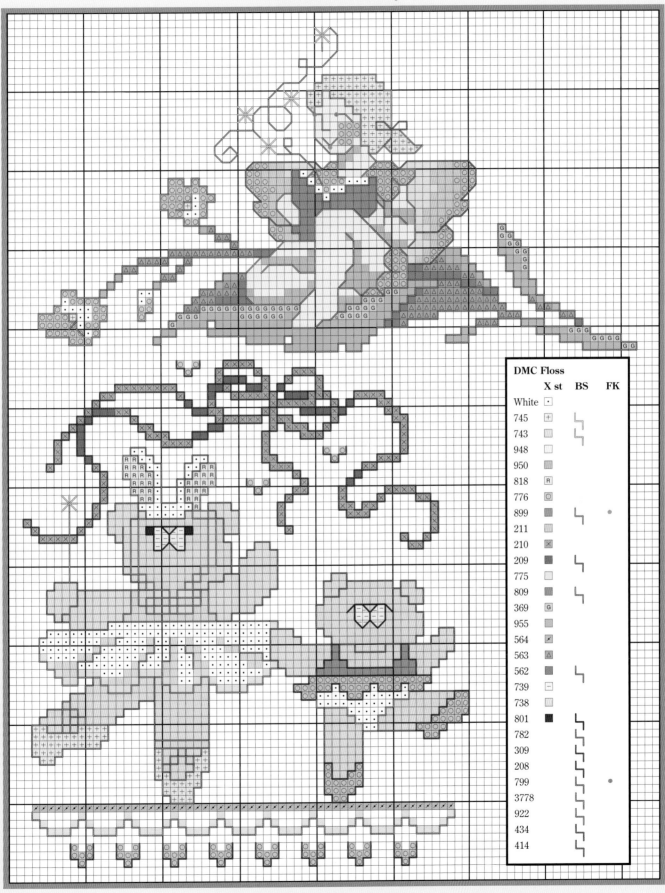

DMC Floss

	X st	BS	FK
White	·		
745	+	⌐	
743		⌐	
948			
950			
818	R		
776	◎		
899		⌐	•
211			
210	✕		
209		⌐	
775			
809		⌐	
369	G		
955			
564	✓		
563	△		
562		⌐	
739	−		
738			
801		⌐	
782		⌐	
309		⌐	
208		⌐	
799		⌐	•
3778			
922		⌐	
434		⌐	
414			

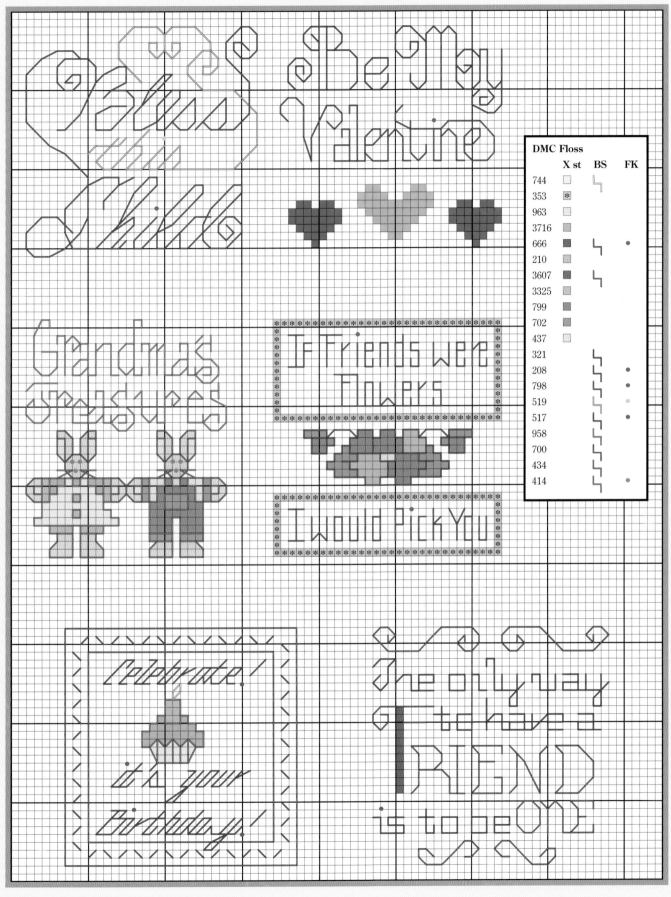

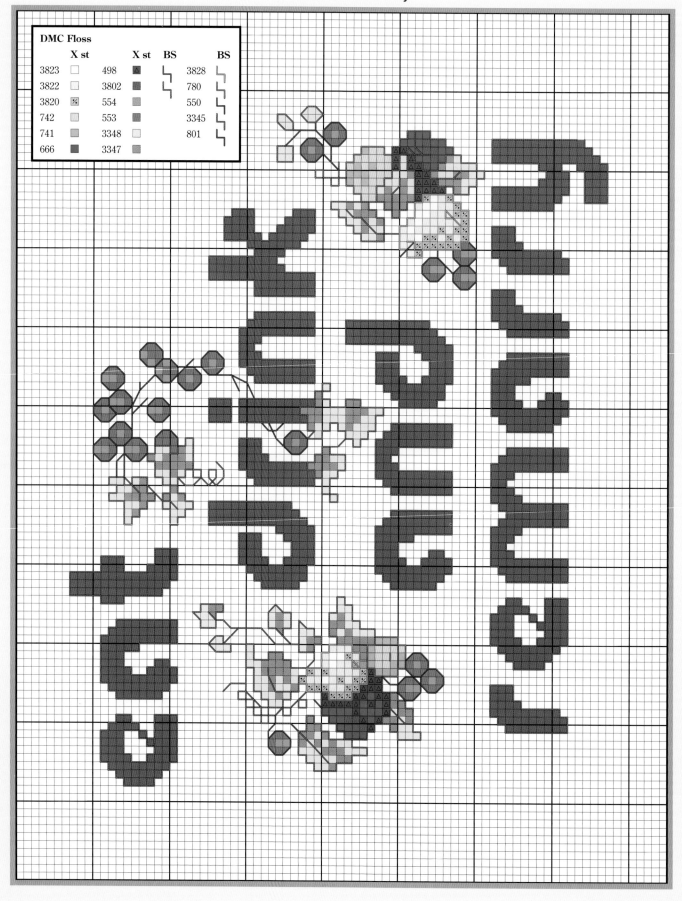

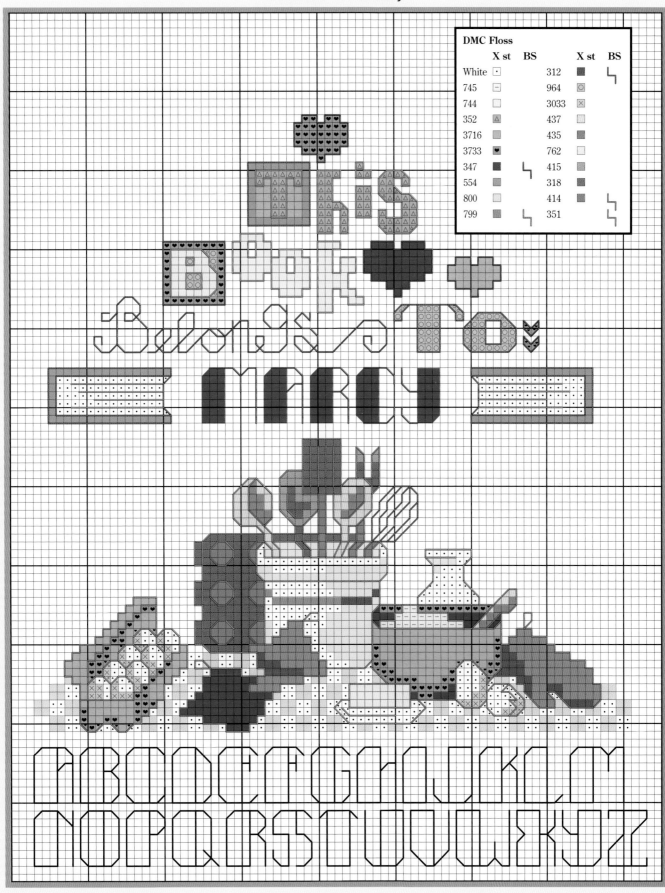

Friends & Family

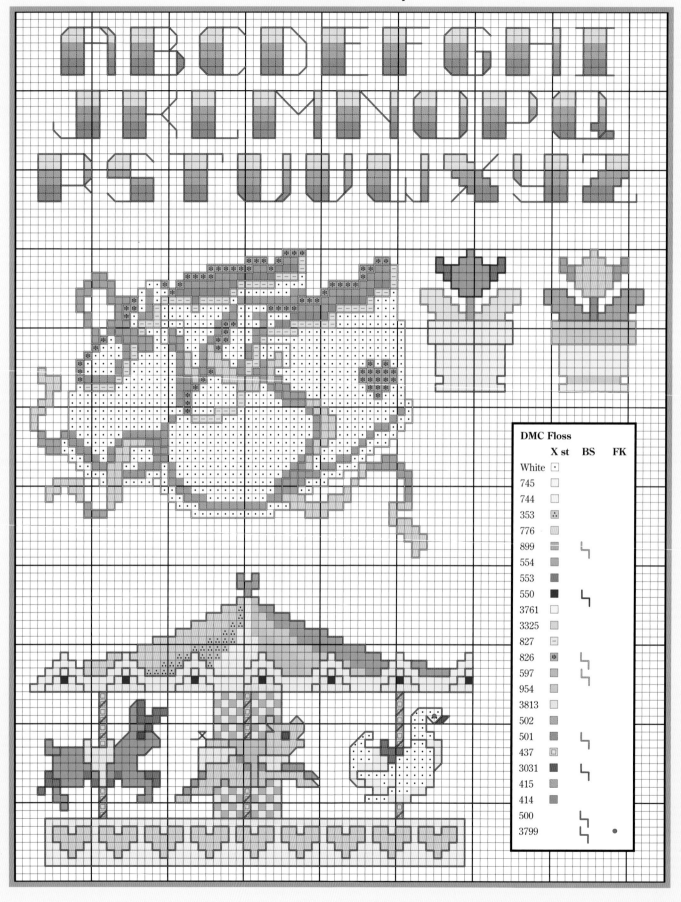

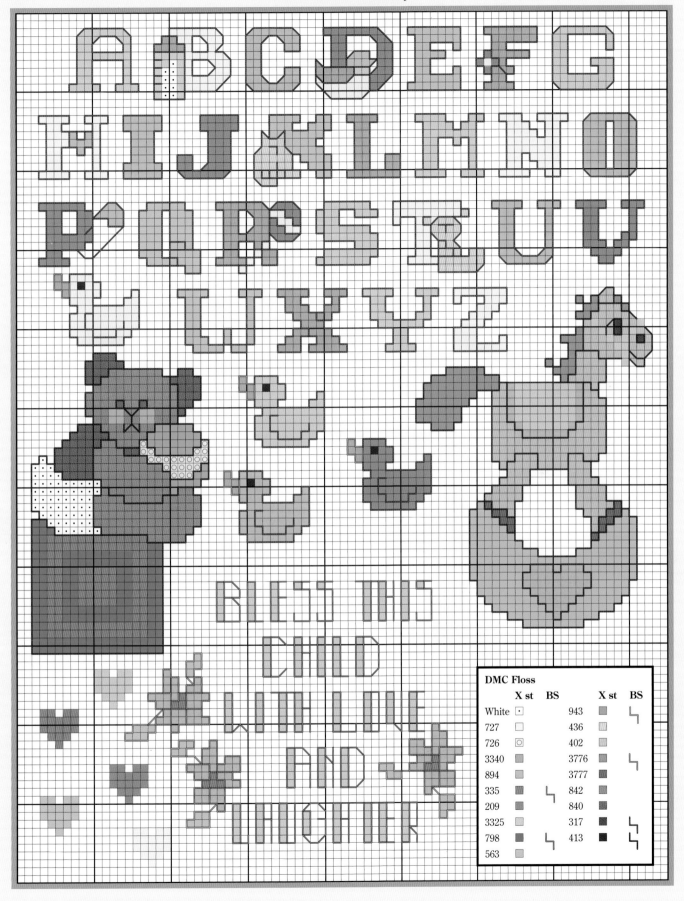

BLESS THIS CHILD WITH LOVE AND LAUGHTER

DMC Floss

	X st	BS		X st	BS
White	·		943		
727			436		⌐
726	⊙		402		
3340			3776		⌐
894			3777		
335		⌐	842		
209			840		
3325			317		⌐
798		⌐	413		⌐
563					

Heart
& Soul

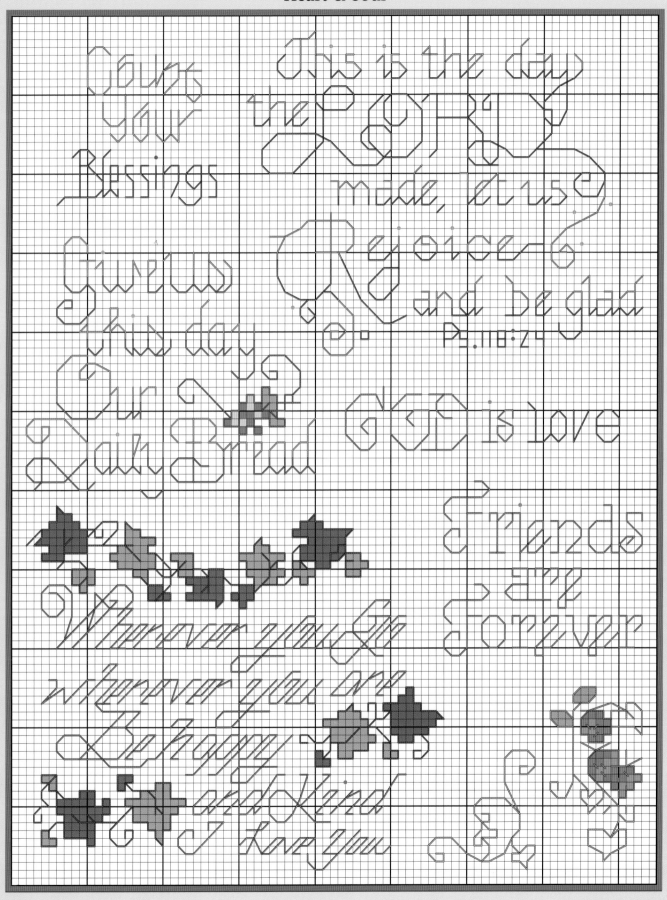

48

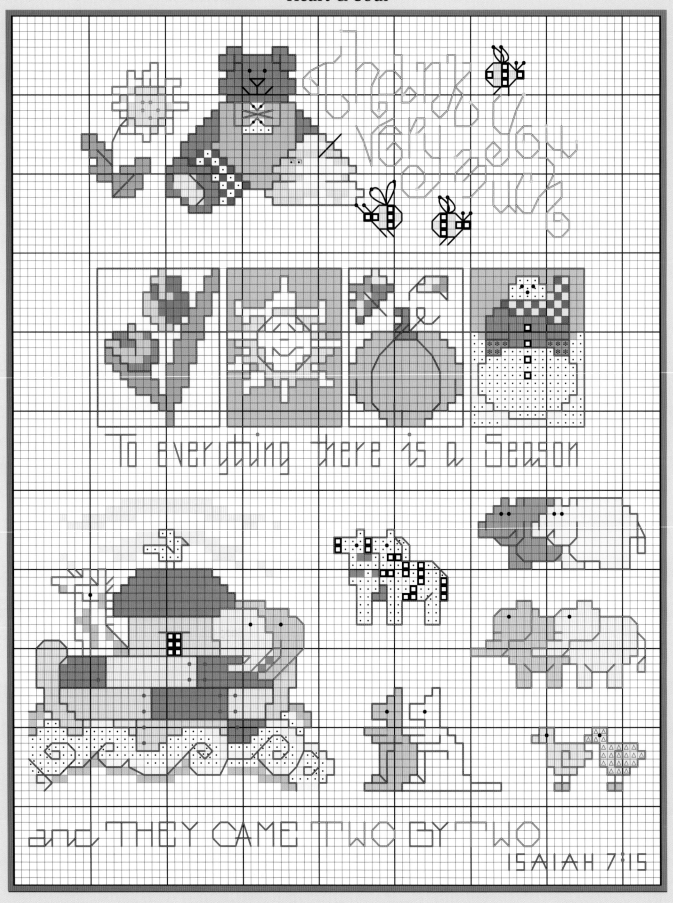

To everything there is a Season

and THEY CAME TWO BY TWO

ISAIAH 7:15

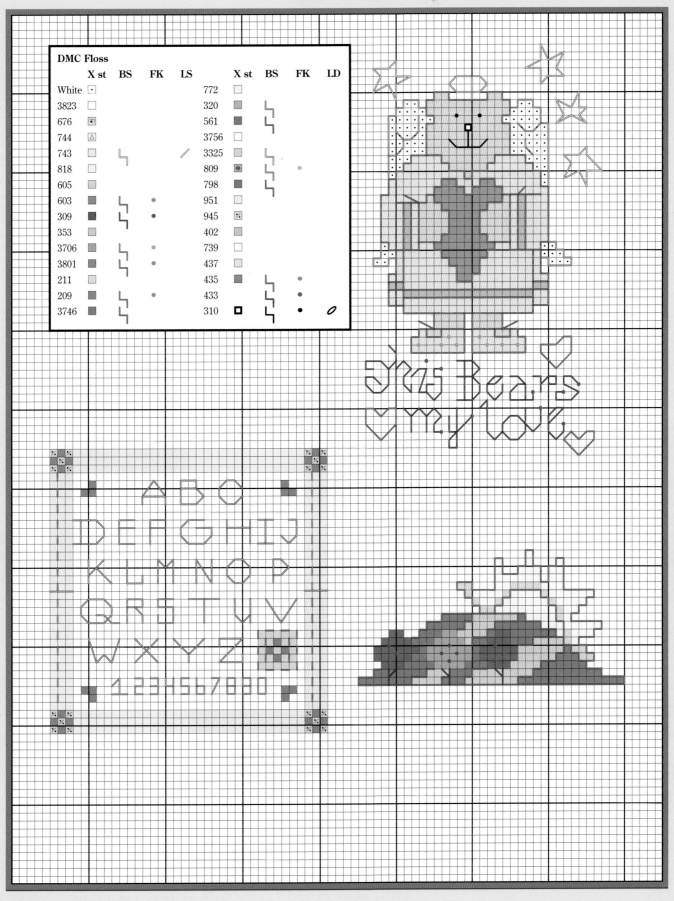

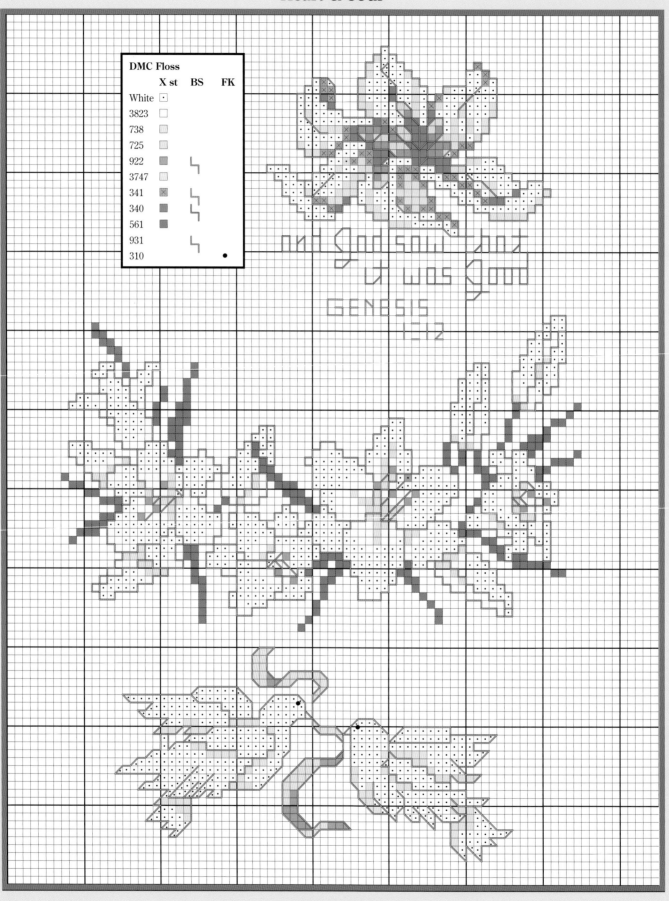

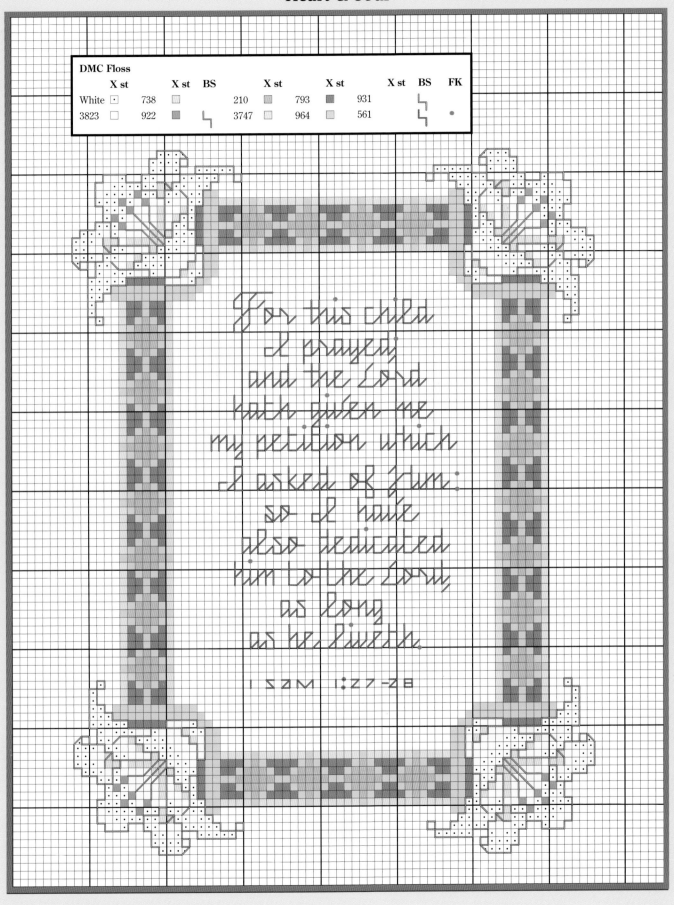

DMC Floss

	X st		X st	BS		X st		X st		X st	BS	FK
White	·	738				210		793		931		
3823		922				3747		964		561		·

For this child
I prayed;
and the Lord
hath given me
my petition which
I asked of him:
so I have
also dedicated
him to the Lord,
as long
as he liveth.

I SAM 1:27-28

51

Heart & Soul

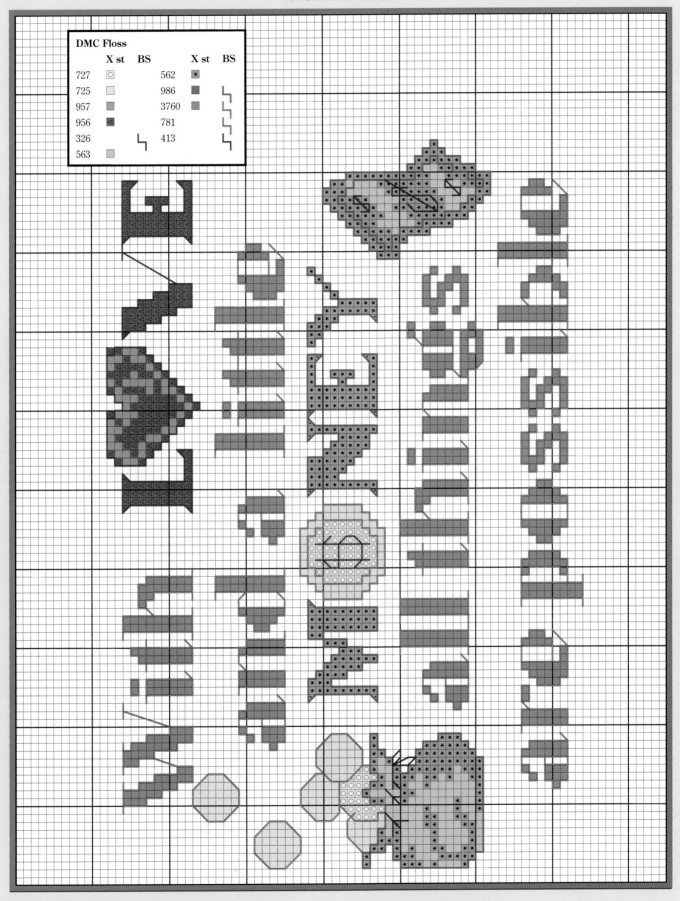

DMC Floss

	X st	BS
White	·	
745		
353		
352		⌐
347		⌐
818	△	
776	S	
899		
315		⌐
964		
368	+	
367	♥	⌐
3013	○	
3052		
3362		⌐
762		
318		⌐
317		⌐

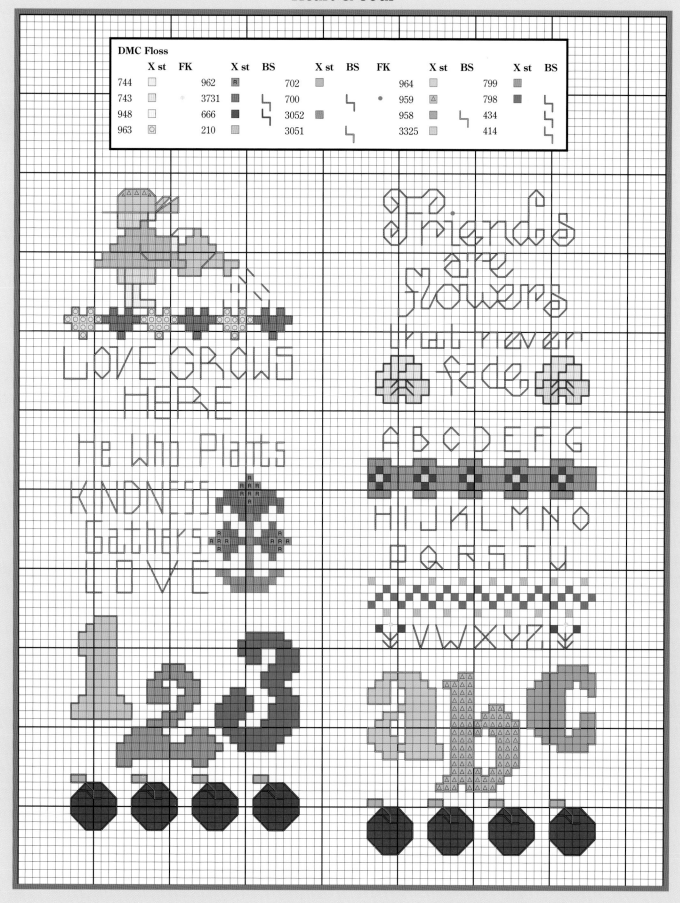

DMC Floss

	X st	BS	FK
White	⊡		
745			
744			
743			
3716			
3731		∟	•
321			
3609			
3608	♥		
3607		∟	
210			
209		∟	
704			
702		∟	
959	○		
3325			
799		∟	•
783		∟	
435		∟	
414		∟	
310	★	∟	•

Heart & Soul

DMC Floss			
	X st	BS	FK
White			
744			
743		⌐	
353		⌐	
818			
3716		⌐	•
3731		⌐	
321			
3609		⌐	
954		⌐	
964			
959			
958		⌐	
3761			
3325			
517		⌐	
798		⌐	
739			
738			
783			
780		⌐	
414			

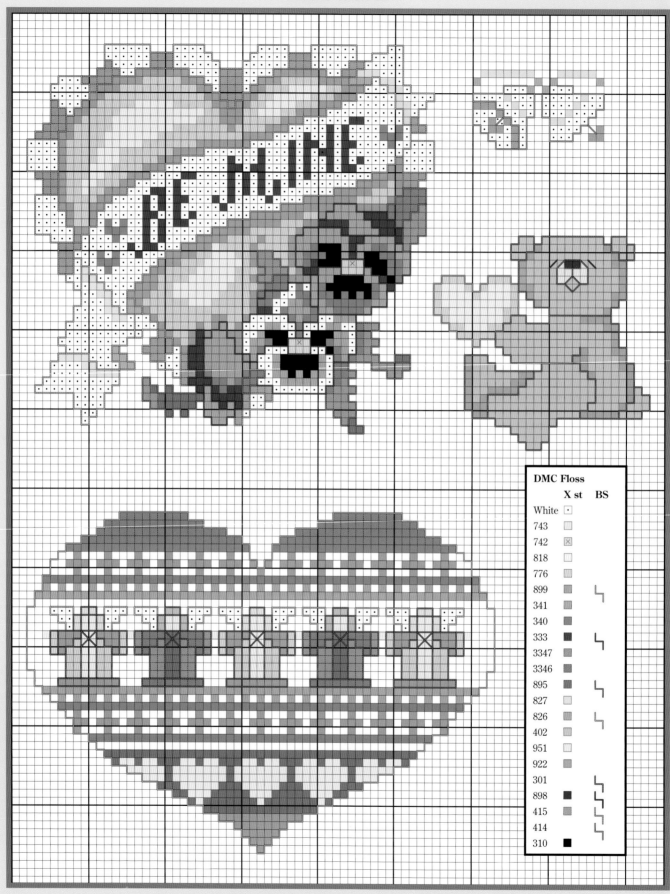

DMC Floss		
	X st	BS
White	·	
743		
742	⊠	
818		
776		
899		⌐
341		
340		
333		⌐
3347		
3346		
895		⌐
827		⌐
826		
402		
951		
922		
301		⌐
898		⌐
415		⌐
414		⌐
310		⌐

Heart & Soul

Hearth
&
Home

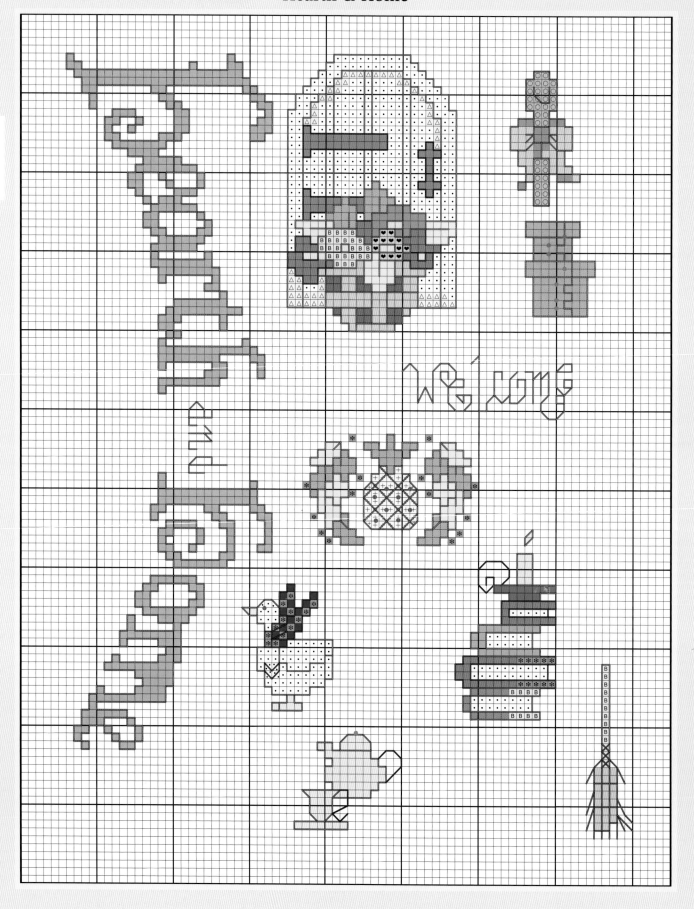

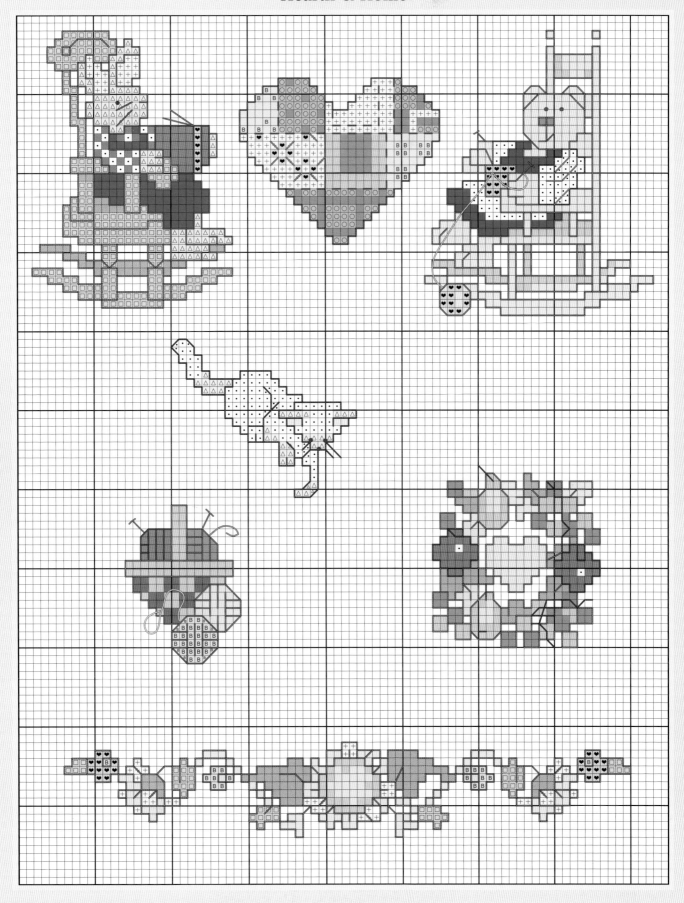

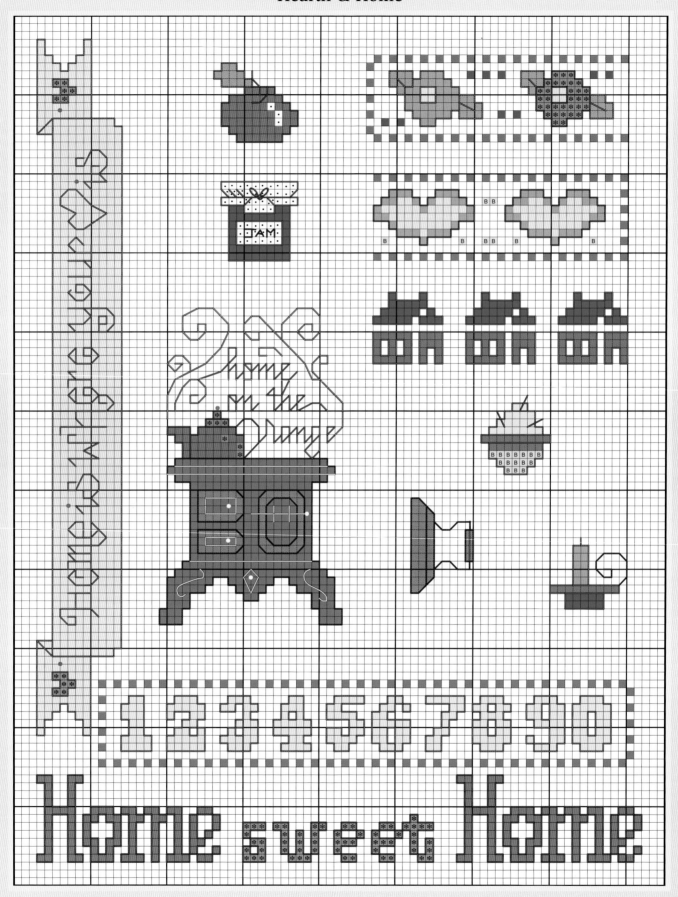

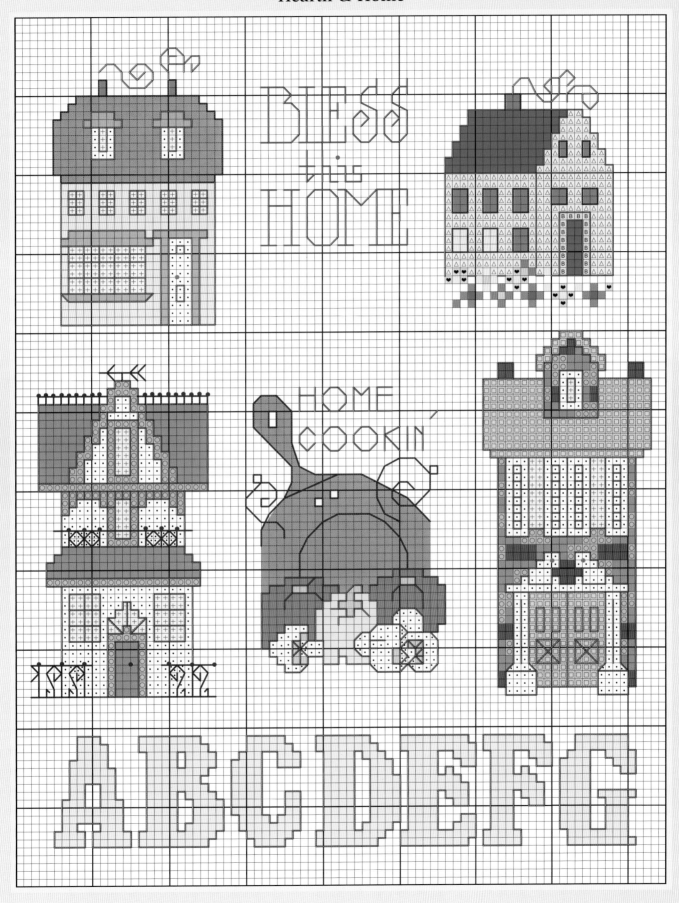

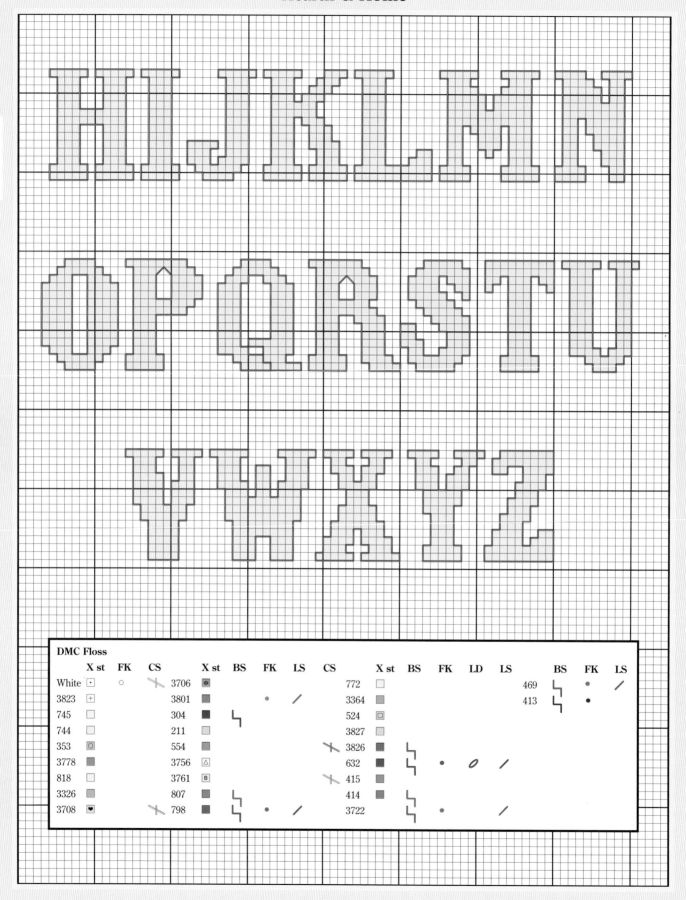

DMC Floss

	X st	FK	CS		X st	BS	FK	LS	CS		X st	BS	FK	LD	LS		BS	FK	LS
White	·	○	✕	3706	✳					772						469	⌐	•	/
3823	+			3801	▨		•	/		3364						413	⌐	•	
745				304	▩	⌐				524	⊡								
744				211	▦					3827	▥								
353	⊙			554	▨				✕	3826	▨	⌐							
3778				3756	△					632	▨	⌐	•	0	/				
818				3761	B				✕	415	▨								
3326				807	▨	⌐				414	▨	⌐							
3708	❤		✕	798	▨	⌐	•	/		3722	▨	⌐	•		/				

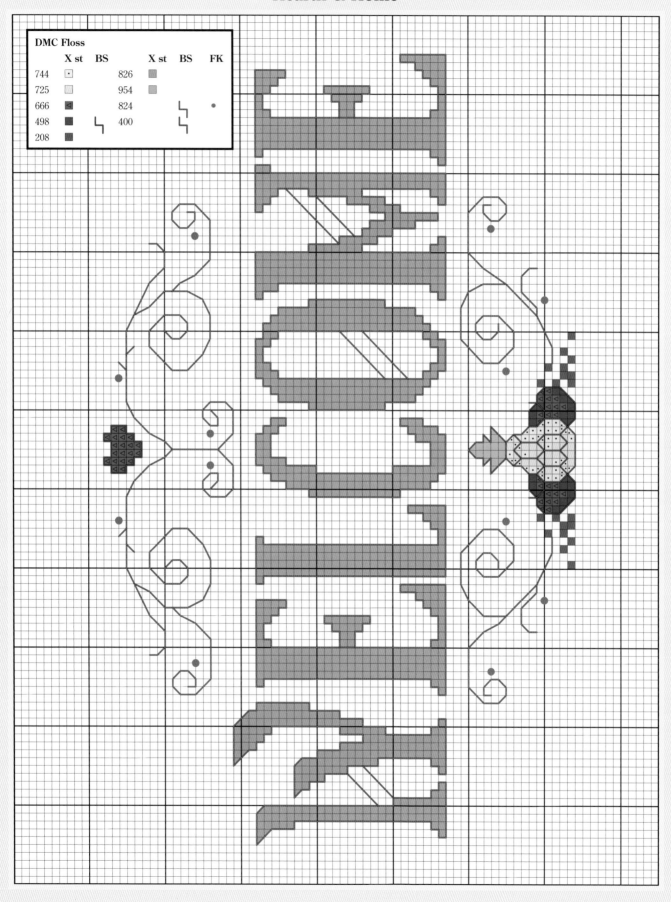

DMC Floss

	X st	BS		X st	BS	FK
744	·		826			
725			954			
666	◁		824			
498		⌐	400		⌐	
208						•

DMC Floss

	X st	BS		X st	BS
White	·		3685		⌐
3078			3753		
3822			3325		
783			799		
780		⌐	798		
722			3348		
721			471		
720	▲	⌐	3347	G	⌐
353	M		469		
352			369	⧄	
351			989		
349	✖	⌐	987		⌐
817	▣	⌐	840		
3326	⁙		839		⌐
899	⊠	⌐	3799		⌐
3689			797		⌐
3687			319		⌐

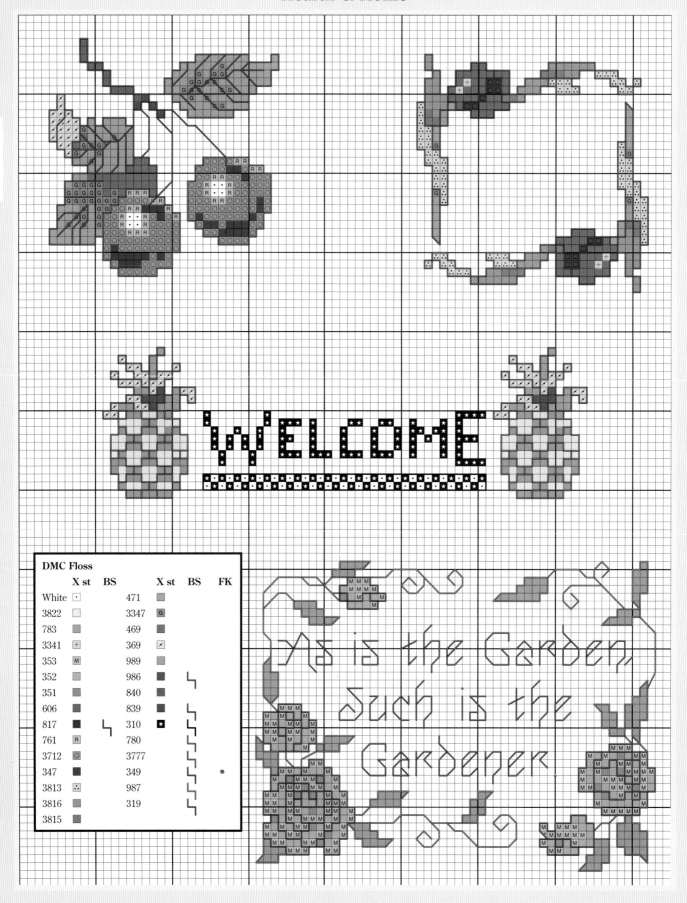

Hearth & Home

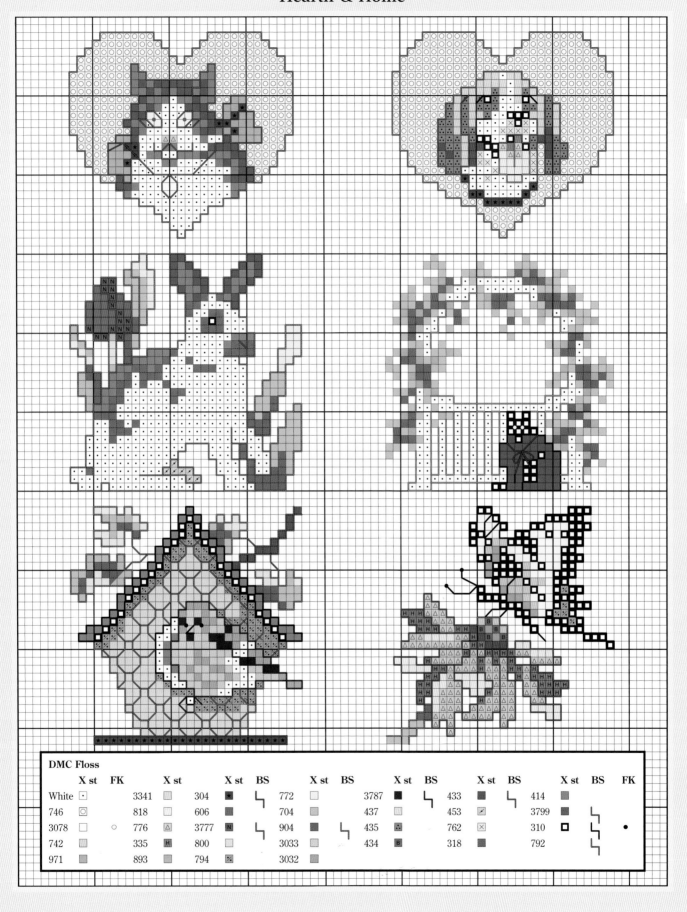

DMC Floss

	X st	FK		X st		X st	BS		X st	BS		X st	BS		X st	BS		X st	BS	FK
White	·		3341		304	★	772		3787		433		414								
746	○		818		606		704		437		453		3799								
3078		○	776	△	3777	N	904		435		762	⊠	310	□		•					
742			335	H	800		3033		434		318		792								
971			893		794		3032														

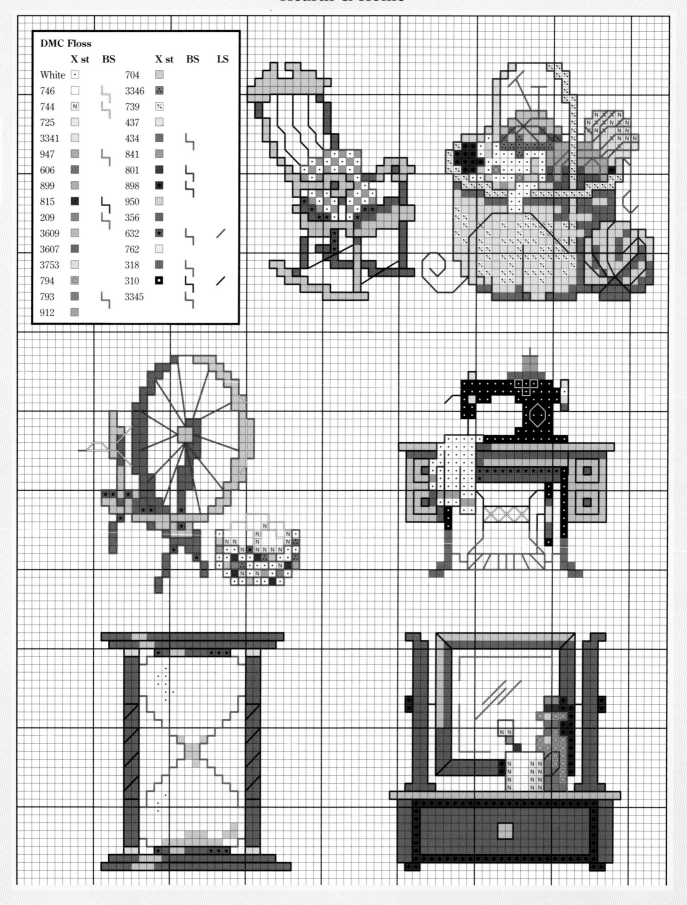

Hearth & Home

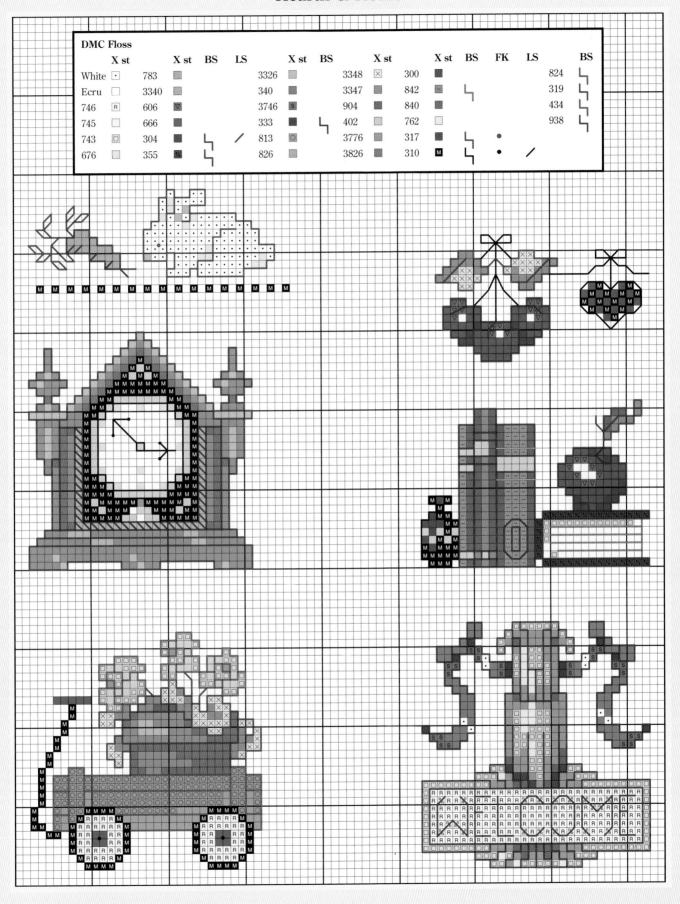

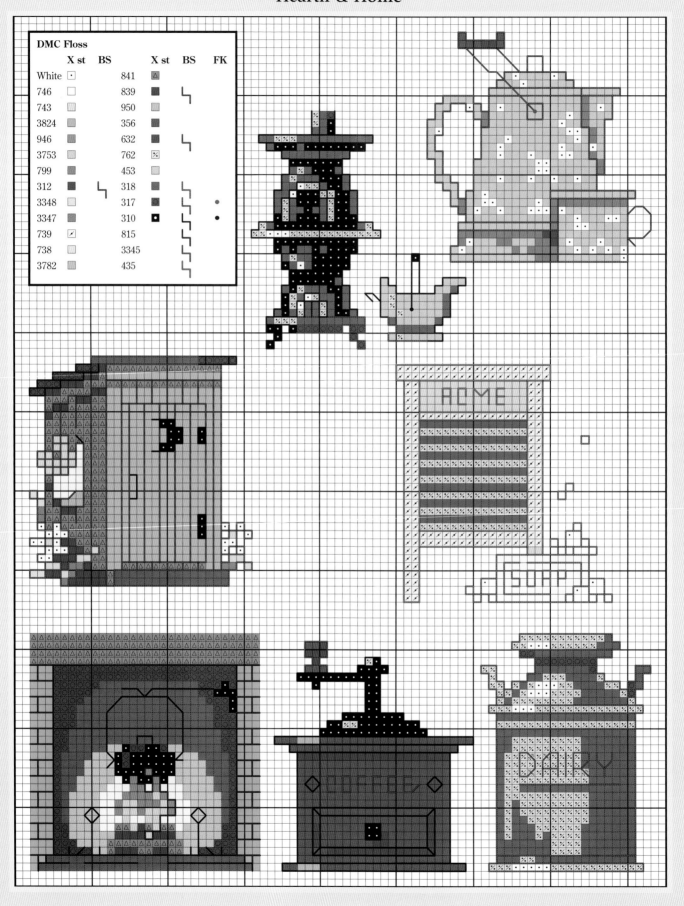

Hearth & Home

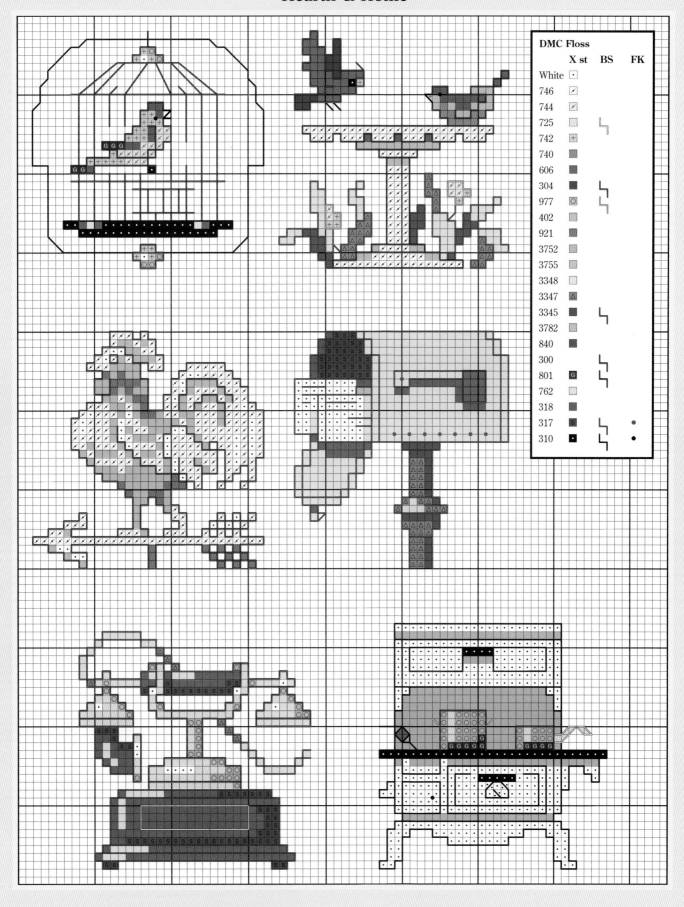

DMC Floss

	X st	BS	FK
White	·		
746			
744			
725		⌐	
742	+		
740			
606			
304		⌐	
977	○	⌐	
402			
921			
3752			
3755			
3348			
3347	△		
3345		⌐	
3782			
840			
300		⌐	
801	G	⌐	
762			
318			
317	S	⌐	•
310	■	⌐	•

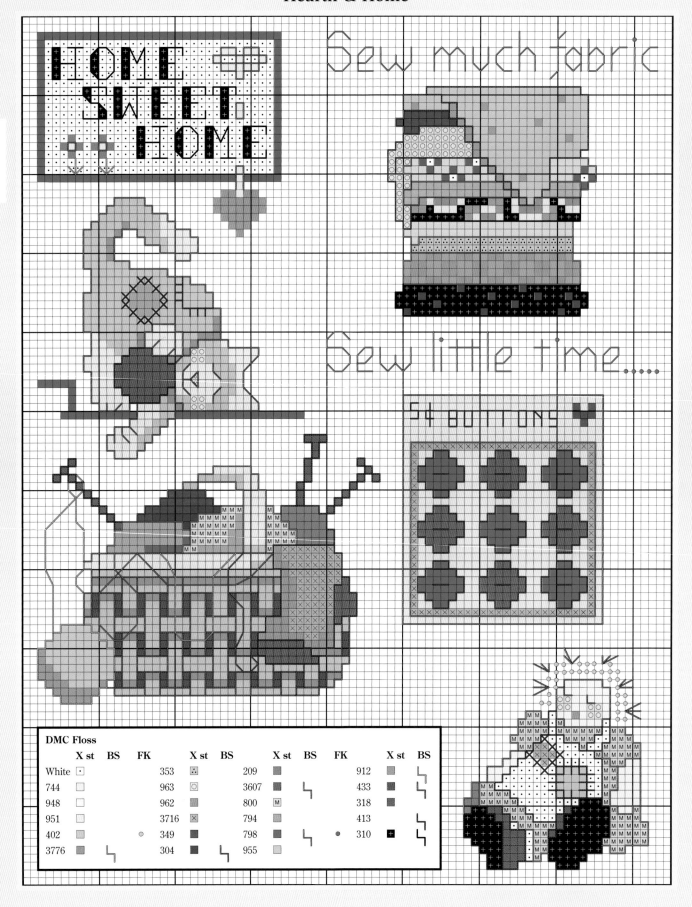

DMC Floss

	X st	BS	FK		X st	BS		X st	BS	FK		X st	BS
White	·			353			209				912		
744				963			3607				433		
948				962			800	M			318		
951				3716			794				413		
402			349			798			310		
3776				304			955						

Hearth & Home

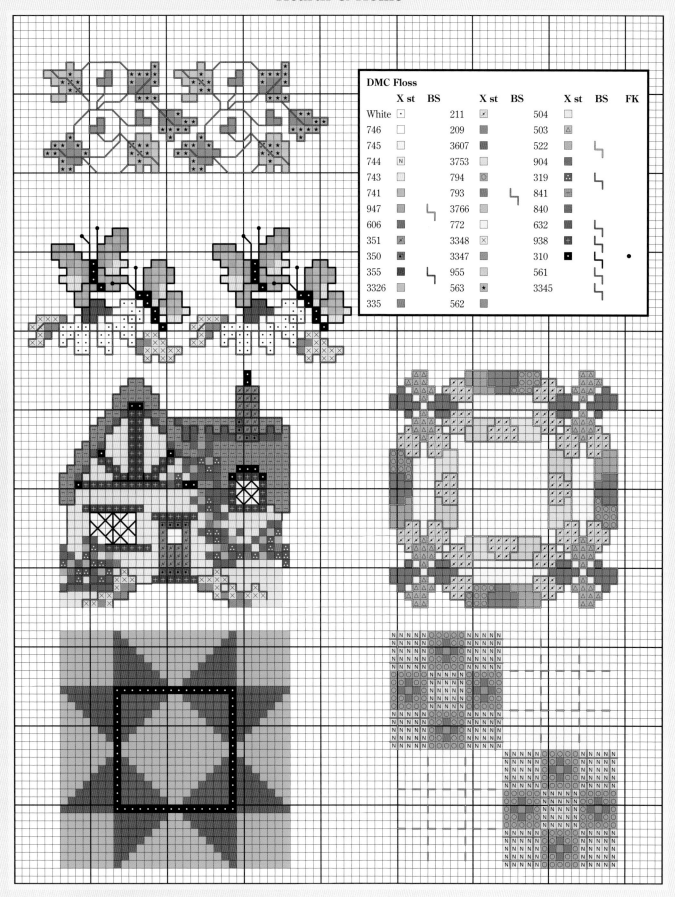

DMC Floss

	X st	BS		X st	BS		X st	BS	FK
White	·		211			504			
746			209			503			
745			3607			522		⌐	
744	N		3753			904			
743			794			319		⌐	
741			793		⌐	841			
947		⌐	3766			840			
606			772			632		⌐	
351			3348			938		⌐	
350			3347			310		⌐	•
355		⌐	955			561		⌐	
3326			563	★		3345		⌐	
335			562					⌐	

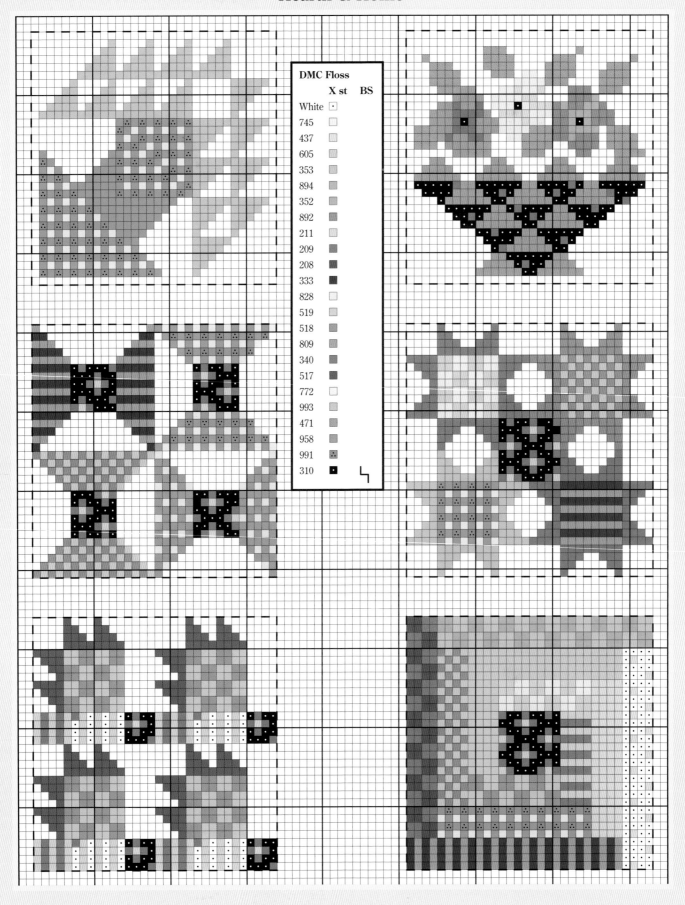

DMC Floss

	X st	BS
White	·	
745		
437		
605		
353		
894		
352		
892		
211		
209		
208		
333		
828		
519		
518		
809		
340		
517		
772		
993		
471		
958		
991		
310		

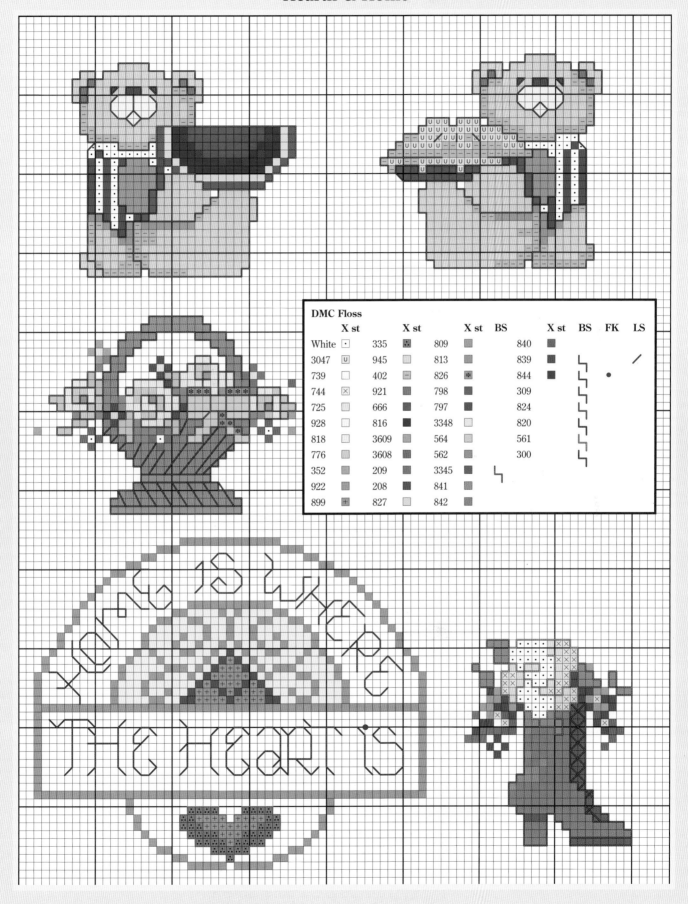

DMC Floss

	X st		X st		X st	BS		X st	BS	FK	LS
White	·	335		809			840				
3047	U	945		813			839				/
739		402		826			844			•	
744	×	921		798			309				
725		666		797			824				
928		816		3348			820				
818		3609		564			561				
776		3608		562			300				
352		209		3345							
922		208		841							
899	+	827		842							

Heaven
&
Nature

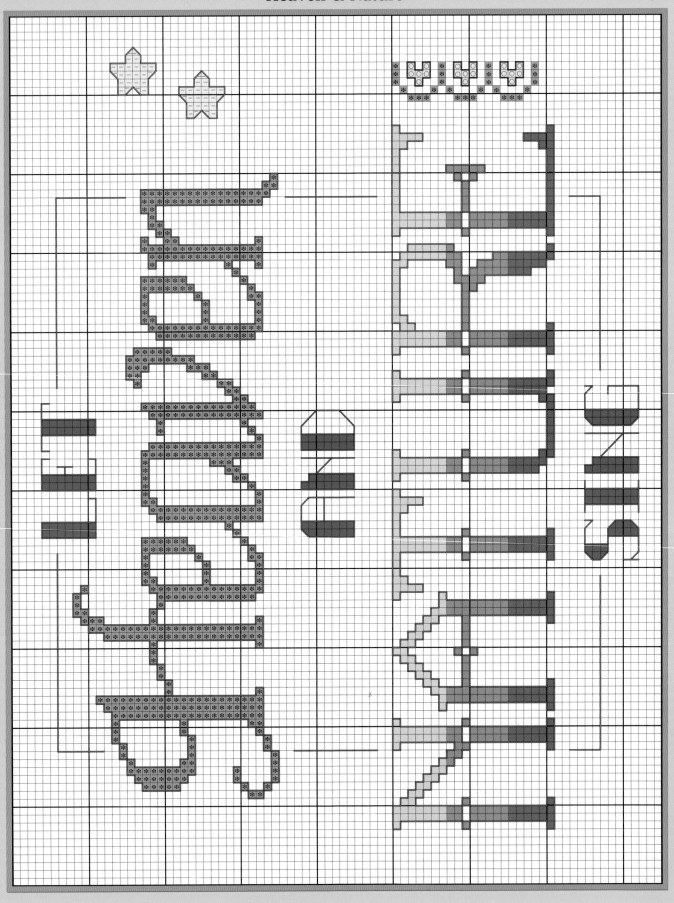

84

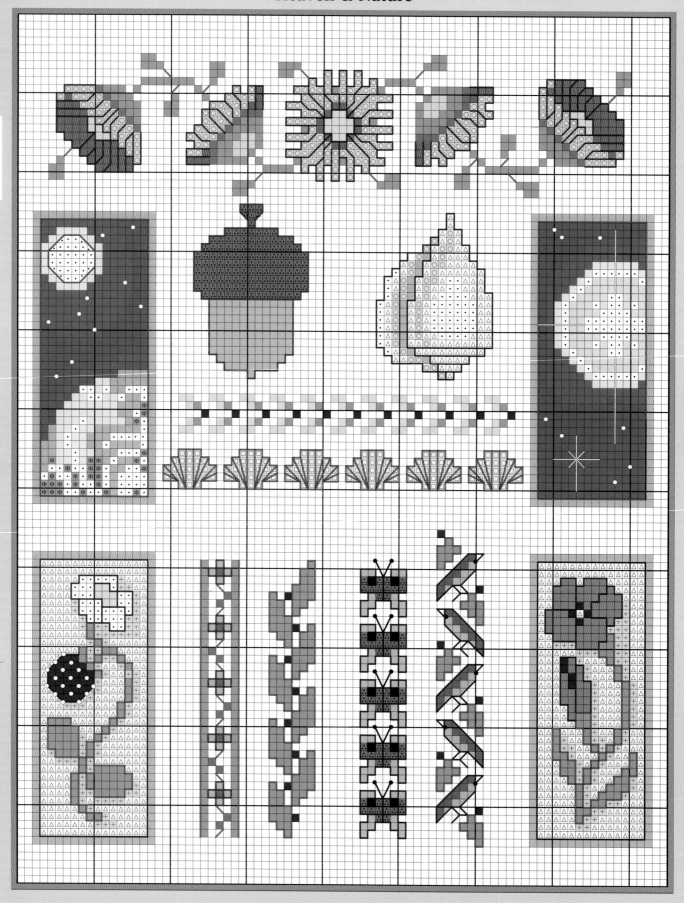

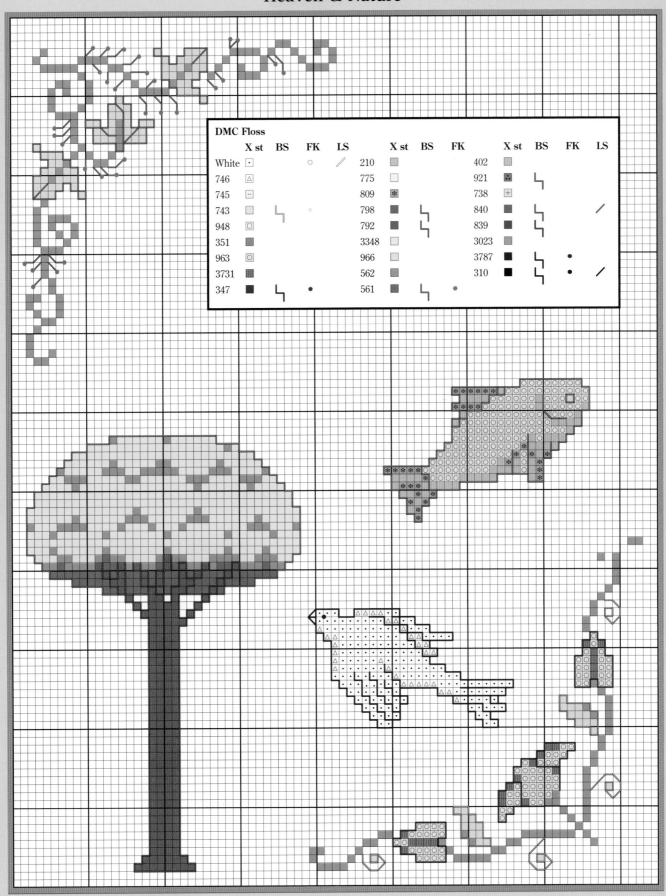

DMC Floss

	X st	BS	FK	LS		X st	BS	FK		X st	BS	FK	LS
White	·		○	/	210				402				
746	△				775				921		⌐		
745	–				809	※			738	+			
743		⌐	·		798		⌐		840		⌐		/
948	□				792		⌐		839		⌐		
351					3348				3023				
963	◎				966				3787		⌐	•	
3731					562				310		⌐	•	/
347		⌐	•		561		⌐	•					

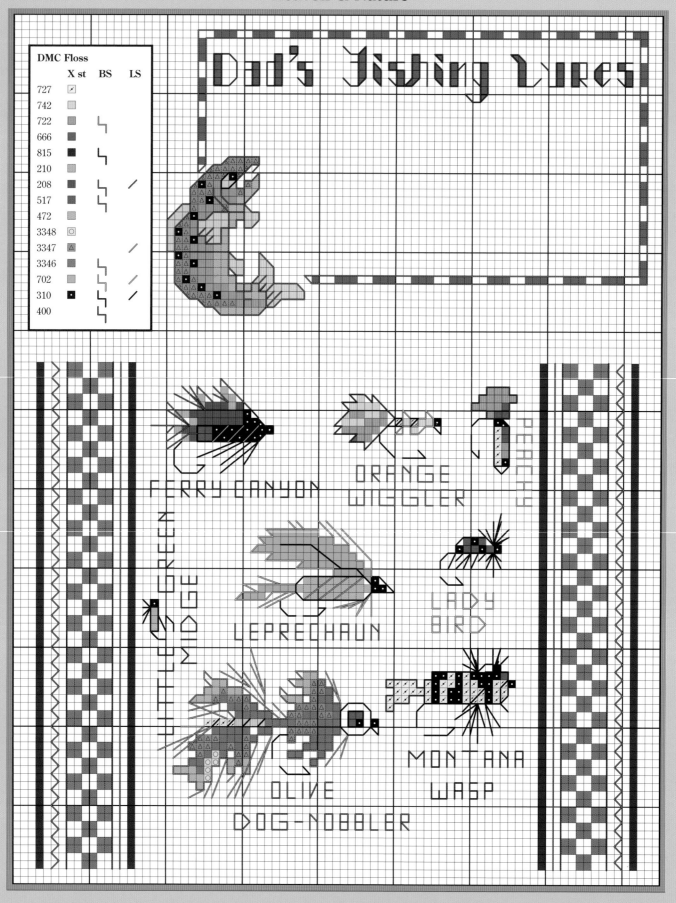

Dad's Fishing Lures

DMC Floss

	X st	BS	LS
727			
742			
722			
666			
815			
210			
208			
517			
472			
3348			
3347			
3346			
702			
310			
400			

8
8

FERRY CANYON

ORANGE WIGGLER

PEACHY

LITTLE GREEN MIDGE

LEPRECHAUN

LADY BIRD

OLIVE DOG-NOBBLER

MONTANA WASP

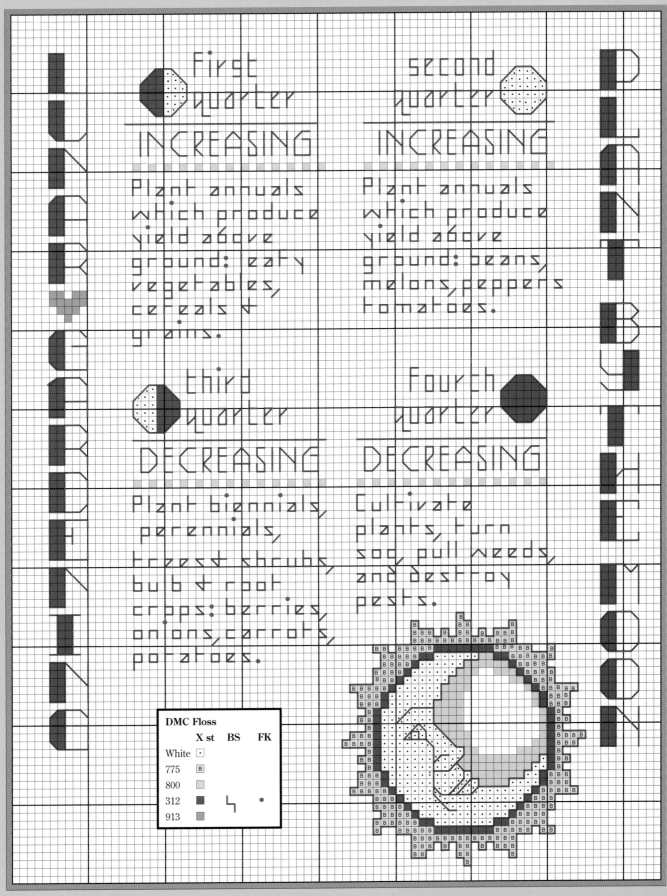

First quarter
INCREASING
Plant annuals which produce yield above ground: leafy vegetables, cereals & grains.

second quarter
INCREASING
Plant annuals which produce yield above ground: beans, melons, peppers tomatoes.

third quarter
DECREASING
Plant biennials, perennials, trees, shrubs, bulb & root crops: berries, onions, carrots, potatoes.

Fourth quarter
DECREASING
Cultivate plants, turn sod, pull weeds, and destroy pests.

DMC Floss

	X st	BS	FK
White	·		
775	B		
800			
312	▨	⌐	•
913	▨		

8
9

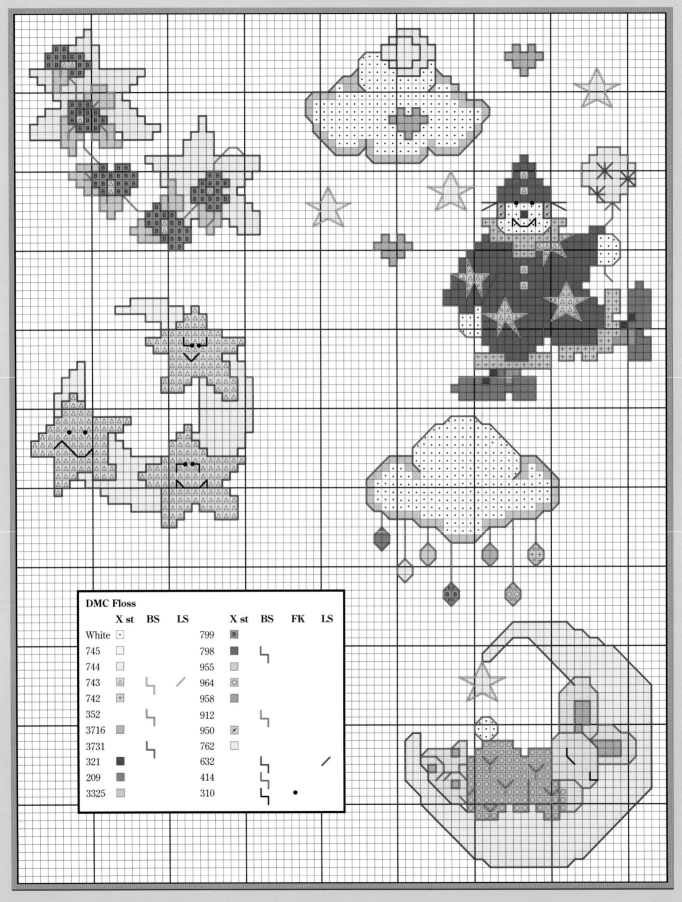

DMC Floss

	X st	BS	LS		X st	BS	FK	LS
White	·			799	B			
745				798		⌐		
744				955				
743	△	⌐	/	964	◎			
742	+			958		⌐		
352		⌐		912		⌐		
3716				950	⊠			
3731		⌐		762				
321				632		⌐		/
209				414		⌐		
3325				310		⌐	•	

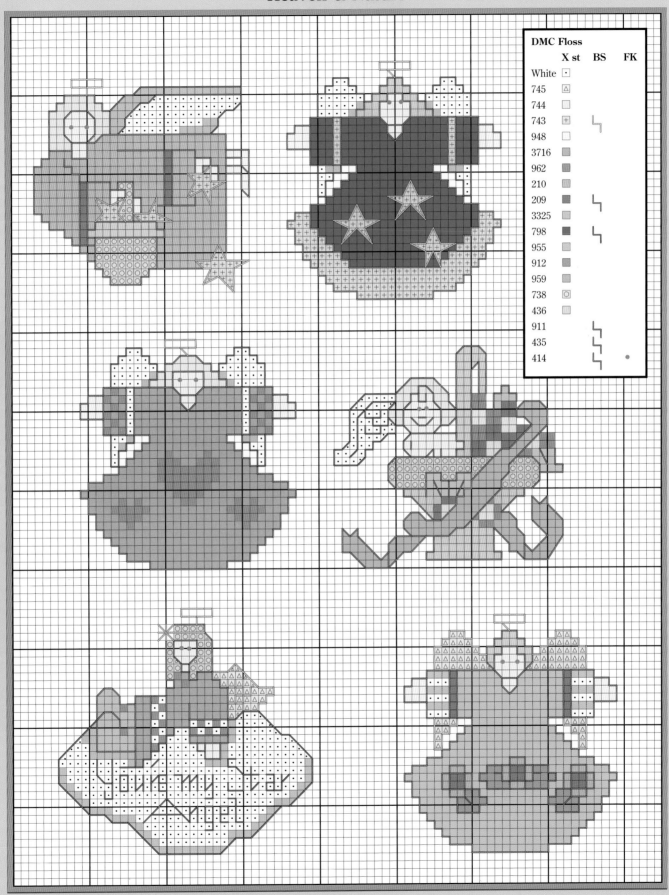

DMC Floss

	X st	BS	FK
White	·		
745	△		
744			
743	+	⌐	
948			
3716			
962			
210			
209		⌐	
3325			
798		⌐	
955			
912			
959			
738	○		
436			
911		⌐	
435		⌐	
414		⌐	·

Heaven & Nature

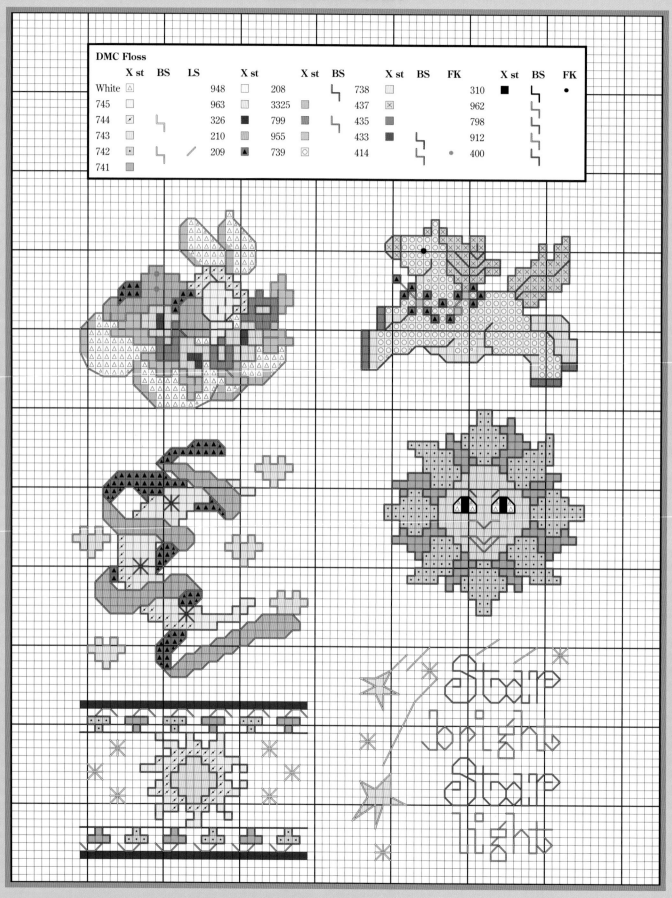

DMC Floss

	X st	BS	LS		X st		X st	BS		X st	BS	FK		X st	BS	FK
White	△			948		208		738			310	■		•
745				963		3325		437	⊠		962			
744				326	■	799		435			798			
743				210		955		433			912			
742	•		/	209	▲	739	◎	414		•	400			
741														

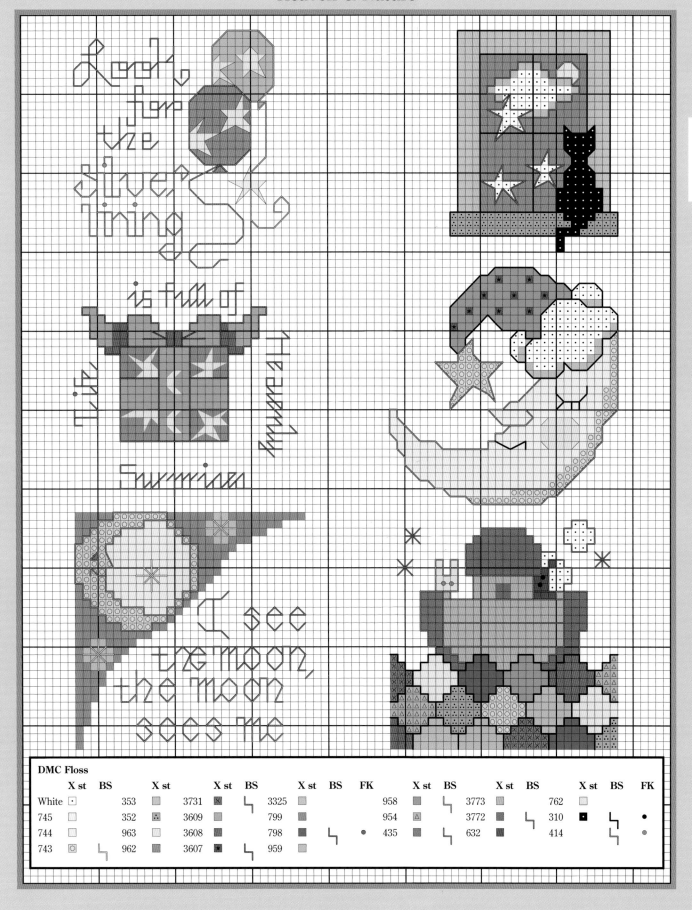

DMC Floss

	X st	BS		X st		X st	BS		X st	BS	FK		X st	BS		X st	BS		X st	BS	FK
White			353			3731			3325				958			3773			762			
745			352			3609			799			954			3772			310			
744			963			3608			798			435			632			414			
743			962			3607			959												

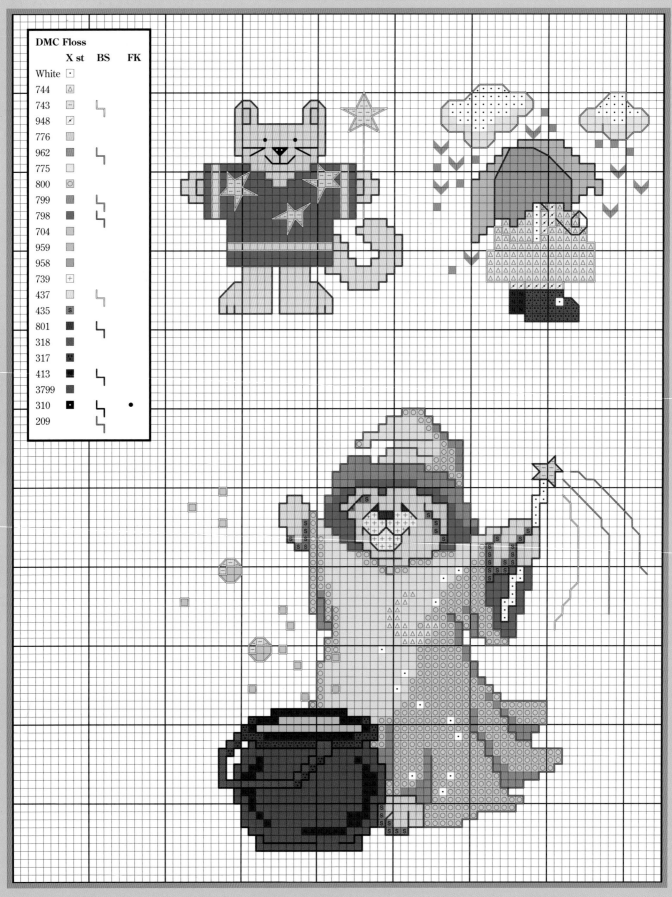

DMC Floss

	X st	BS	FK
White	·		
744	△		
743	⊞	⌐	
948	◿		
776	▨		
962	▨	⌐	
775	▧		
800	◎		
799	▦	⌐	
798	▦	⌐	
704	▦		
959	▦		
958	▦		
739	⊞		
437	▨	⌐	
435	s		
801	▦	⌐	
318	▦		
317	▨		
413	▦	⌐	
3799	▦		
310	▦	⌐	●
209		⌐	

9
6

DMC Floss

	X st		X st	BS
White	·	402		
743	△	922		
740		921	★	
666		300		⌐
209		838	♥	
964		762		
958		415		
702		318		
739	+	413		⌐
738				
437				

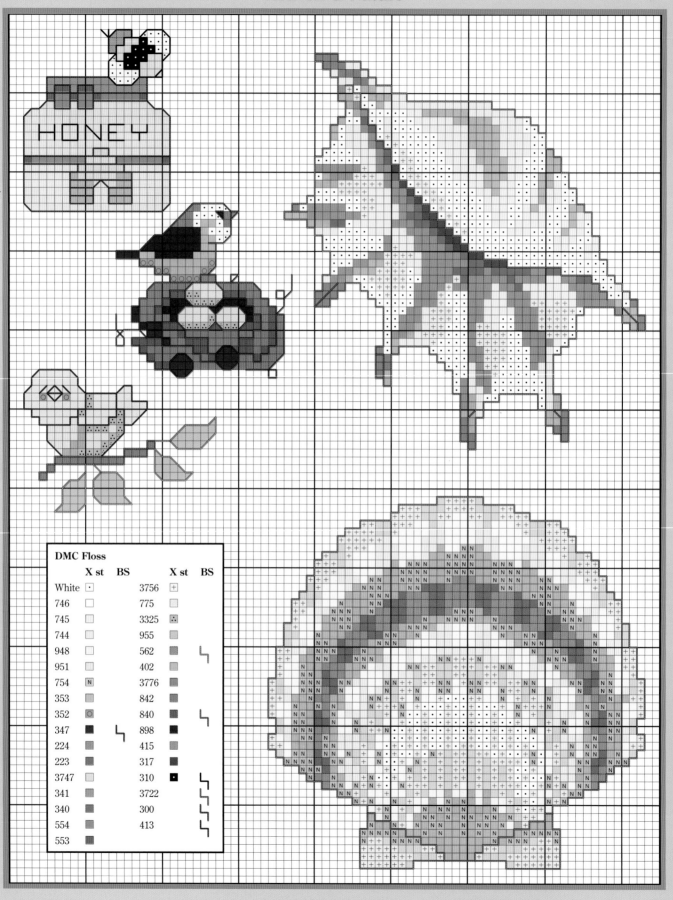

HONEY

DMC Floss

	X st	BS		X st	BS
White	·		3756	+	
746			775		
745			3325		
744			955		
948			562		⌐
951			402		
754	N		3776		
353			842		
352	◎		840		⌐
347		⌐	898		
224			415		
223			317		
3747			310	■	⌐
341			3722		⌐
340			300		⌐
554			413		⌐
553					

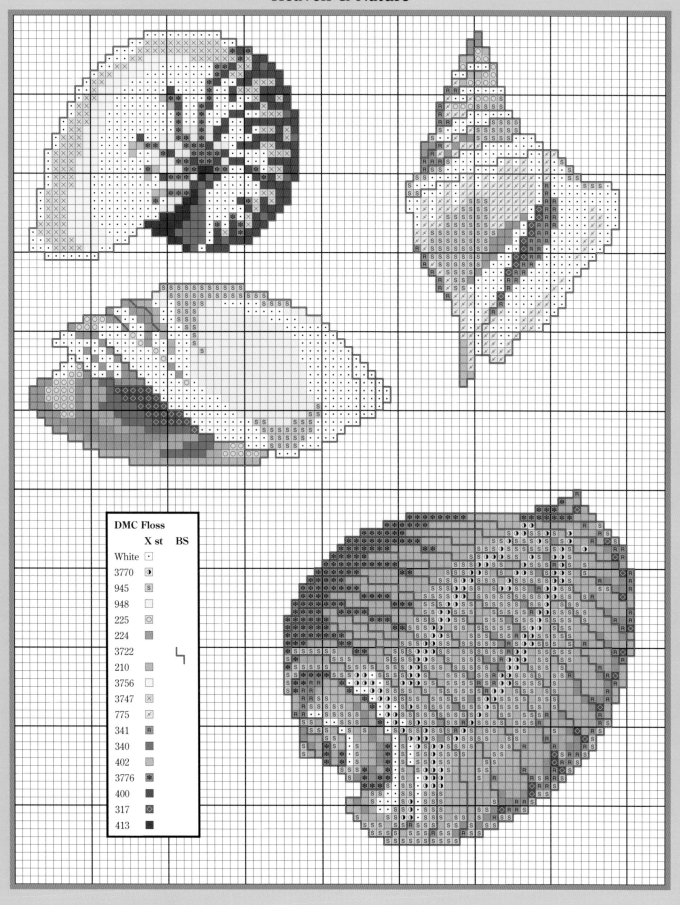

DMC Floss

	X st	BS
White	·	
3770	◉	
945	S	
948	☐	
225	○	
224	▨	
3722		⌐
210	▨	
3756	☐	
3747	☒	
775	⟋	
341	R	
340	▨	
402	▨	
3776	✳	
400	▨	
317	◇	
413	■	

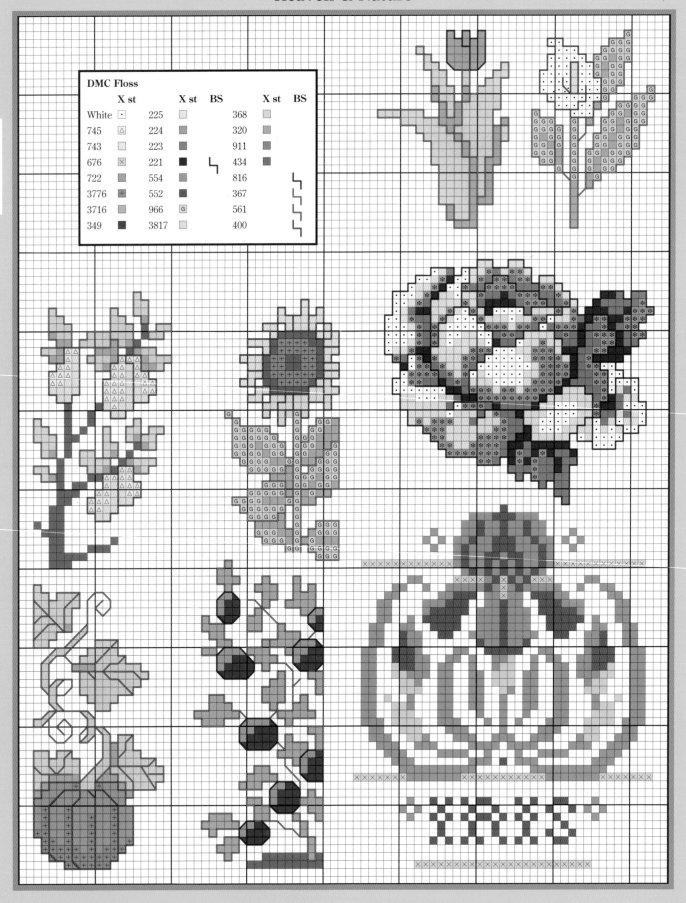

DMC Floss

	X st		X st	BS		X st	BS
White	·	225		368			
745	△	224		320			
743		223		911			
676	✕	221		434	⌐		
722		554		816			
3776	+	552		367			
3716		966	G	561			
349		3817		400			

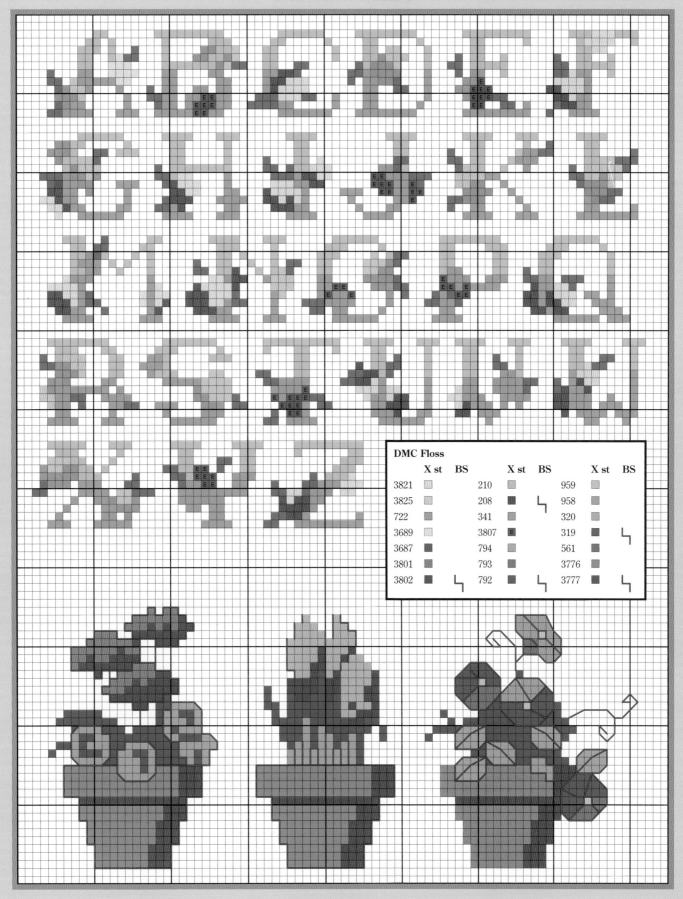

DMC Floss

	X st	BS		X st	BS		X st	BS
3821			210			959		
3825			208		⌐	958		
722			341			320		
3689			3807	E		319		⌐
3687			794			561		
3801			793			3776		
3802		⌐	792		⌐	3777		⌐

Happy
Holidays

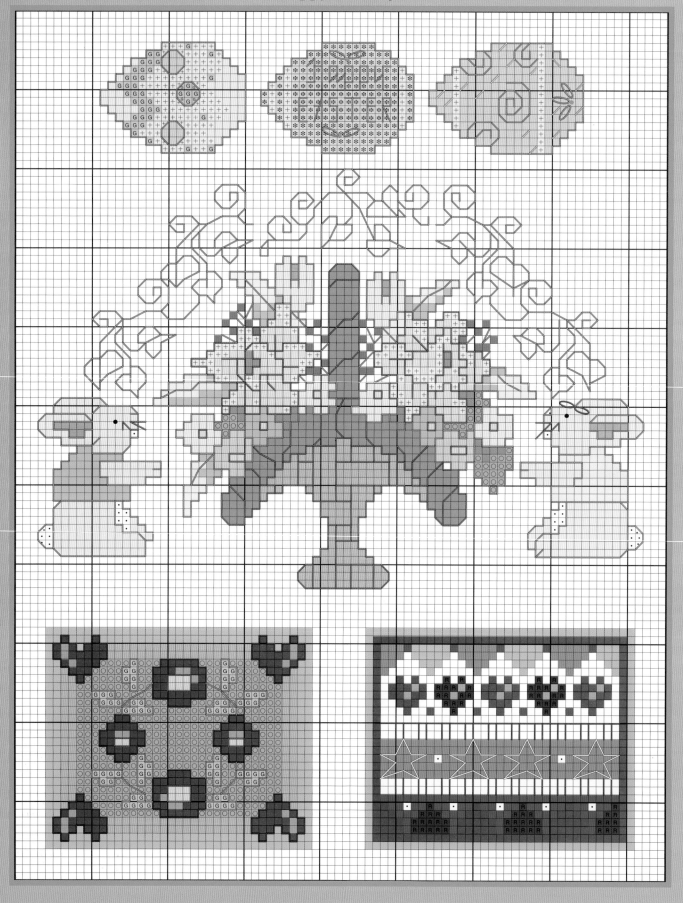

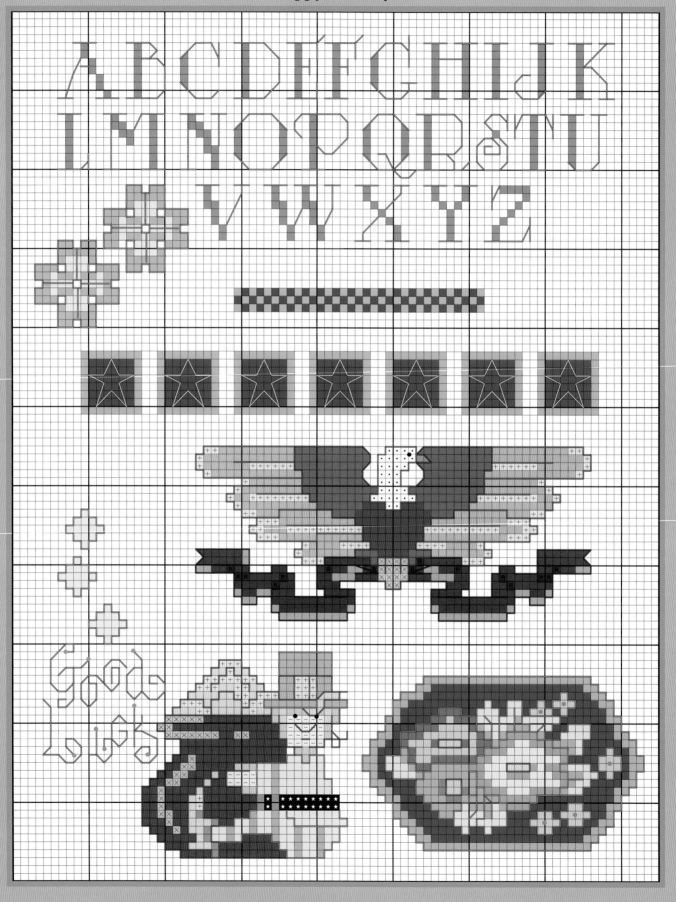

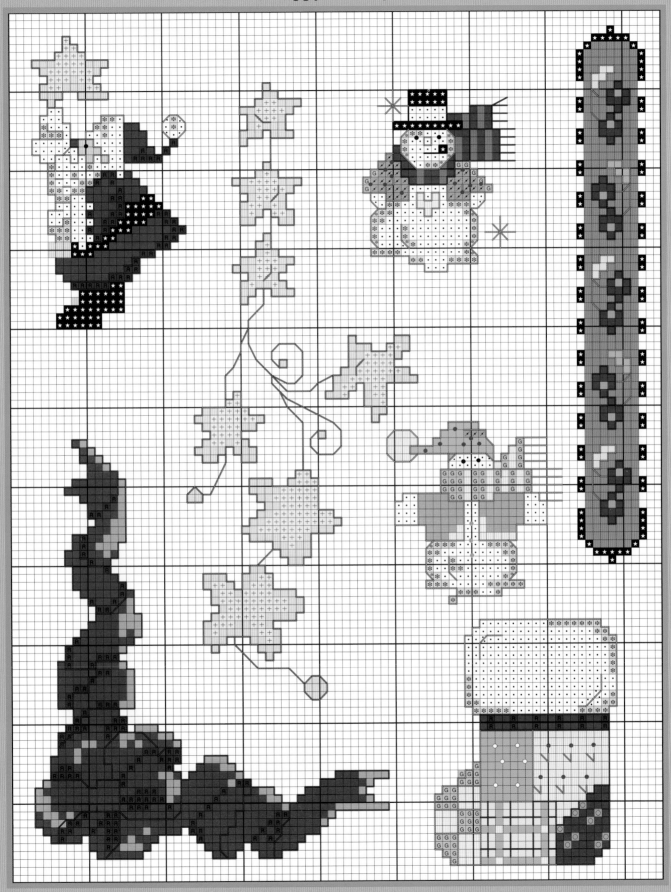

Happy Holidays

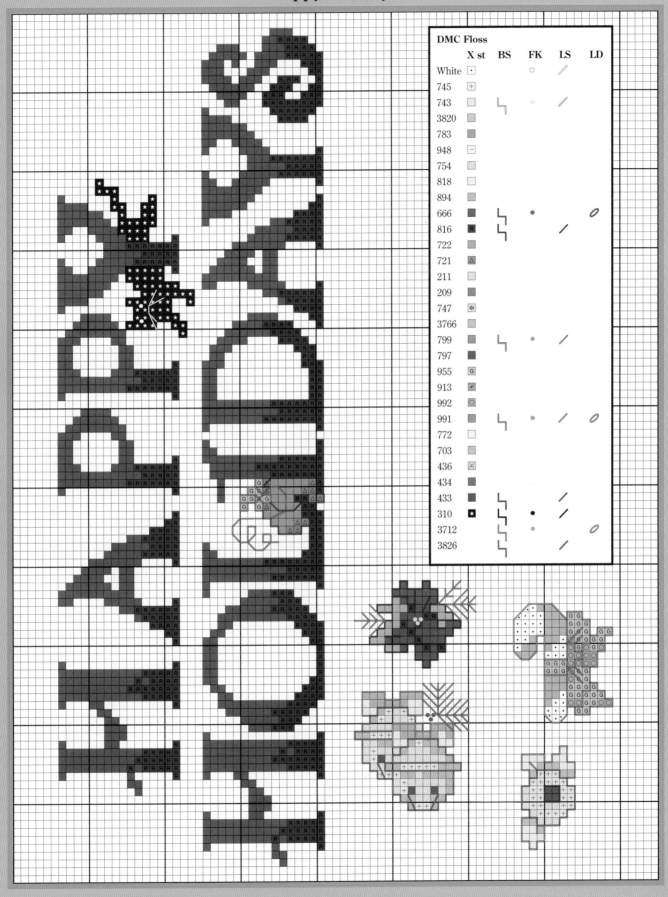

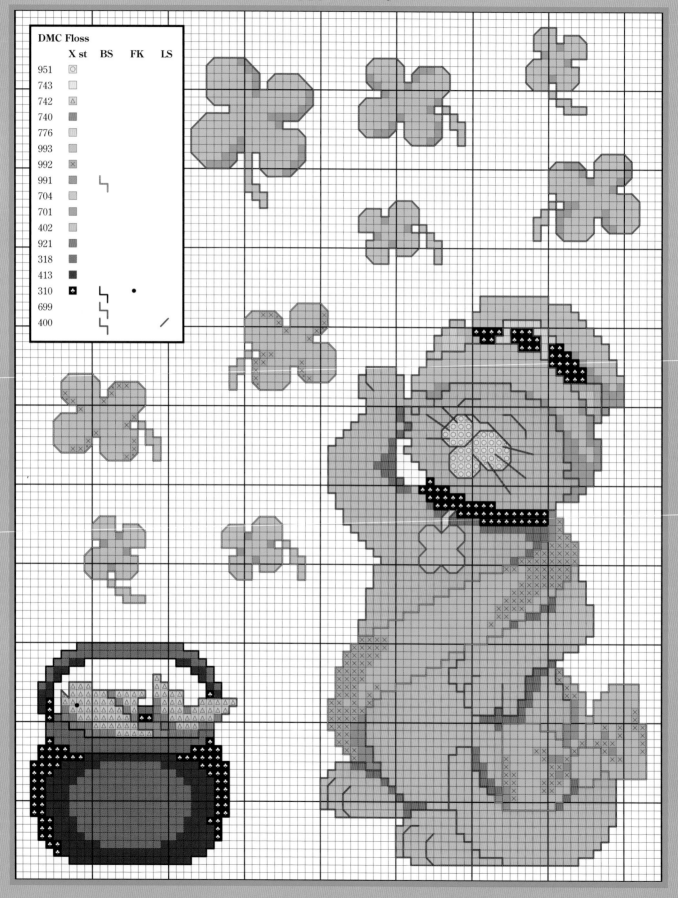

DMC Floss

	X st	BS	FK	LS
951				
743				
742				
740				
776				
993				
992				
991				
704				
701				
402				
921				
318				
413				
310			•	
699				
400				/

110

111

DMC Floss

	X st		X st	BS	LS		X st	BS	FK
White	·	209	✕			413	■	⌐	•
353		208	▨	⌐		310	■	⌐	
963		3761				351		⌐	
3716	R	334				3350		⌐	•
961		959				943		⌐	
211		415		⌐	╱				

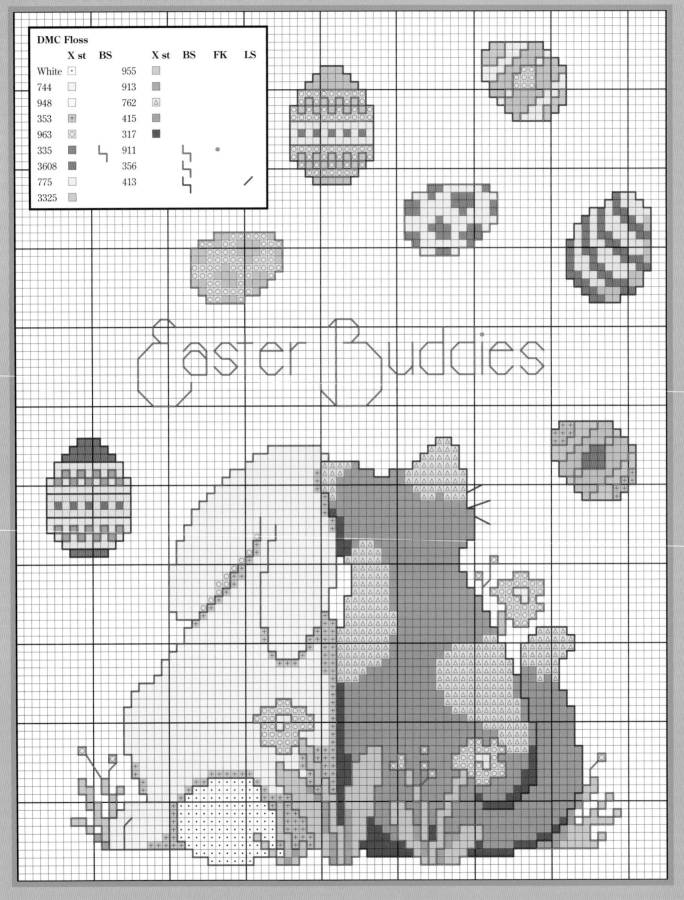

DMC Floss

	X st	BS		X st	BS	FK	LS
White	·		955				
744			913				
948			762	△			
353	+		415				
963	⊙		317				
335			911				
3608			356				
775			413				
3325							

Easter Buddies

112

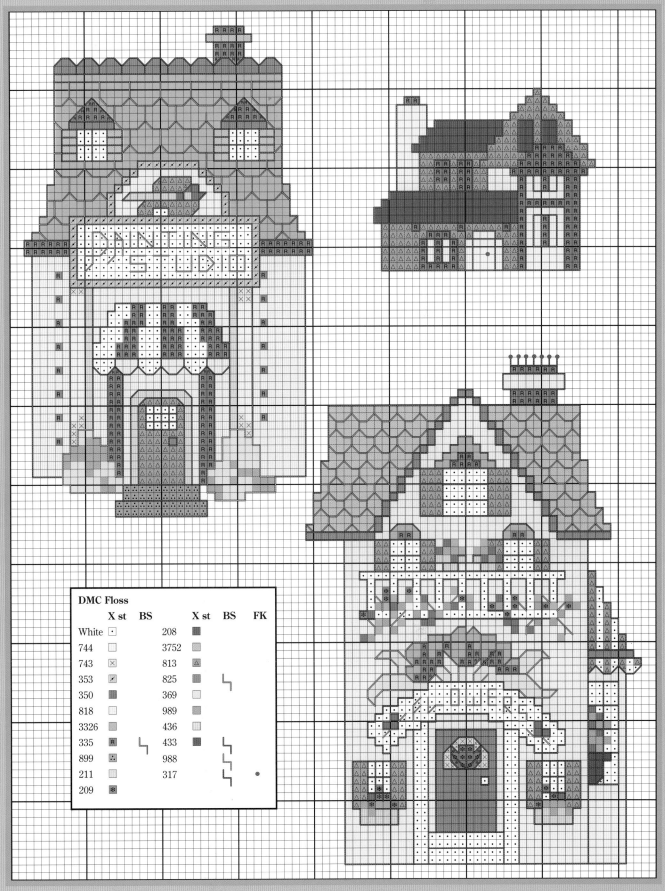

DMC Floss

	X st	BS		X st	BS	FK
White	·		208	■		
744	□		3752	▨		
743	⊠		813	△		
353	◪		825	■	⌐	
350	■		369	□		
818	□		989	■		
3326	▨		436	□		
335	℞	⌐	433	■	⌐	
899	⦂		988	▨	⌐	
211	□		317		⌐	•
209	✳					

Happy Holidays

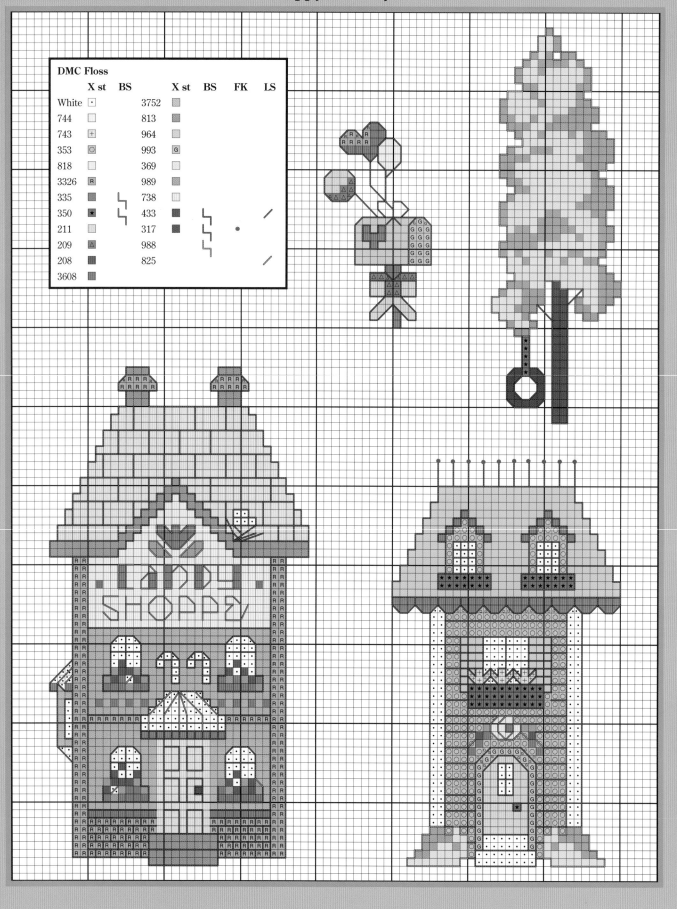

DMC Floss

	X st	BS		X st	BS	FK	LS
White	·		3752				
744			813				
743	+		964				
353	○		993	G			
818			369				
3326	R		989				
335			738				
350	★		433				
211			317			•	
209	△		988				
208			825				
3608							

Happy Holidays

DMC Floss

	X st	BS		X st	BS		X st	BS	FK	LS
White	·		335	E	⌐	989				
746	+		211			738				
744			209			436	×			
743	-		208			433		⌐	•	/
353	R		3608			801		⌐		
352	∴		3752			762				
350		⌐	813	✳		415				
818			825			988			⌐	
3326	◎		964	△		317			•	
899										

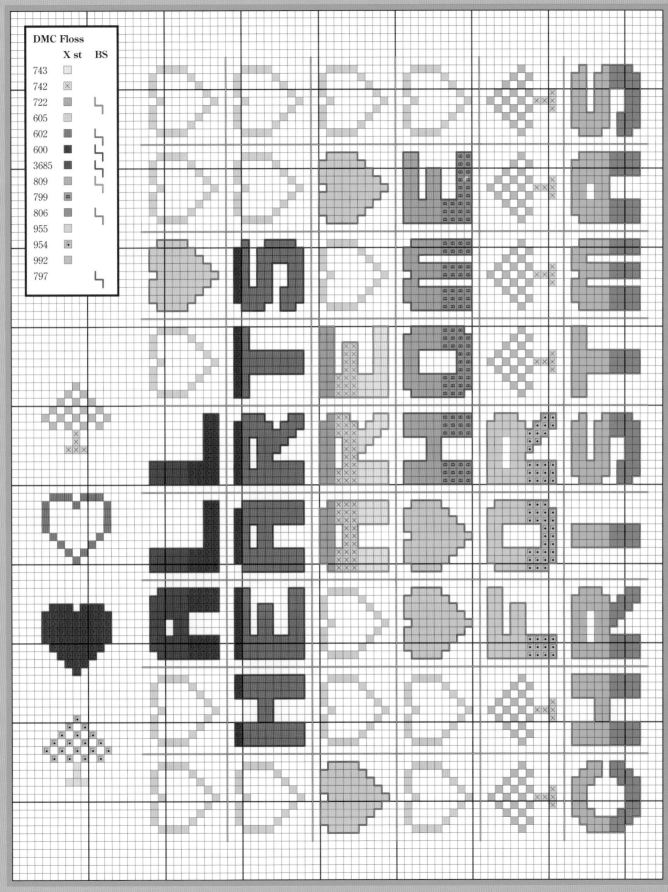

DMC Floss

	X st	BS
743		
742		
722		
605		
602		
600		
3685		
809		
799		
806		
955		
954		
992		
797		

117

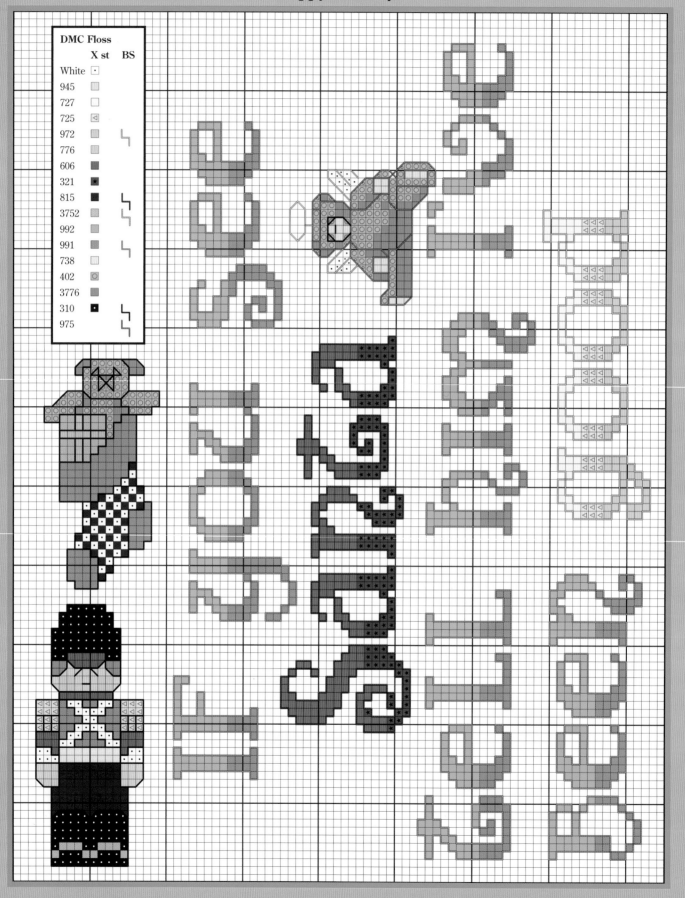

DMC Floss

	X st	BS
White	·	
945		
727		
725	◁	
972		
776		
606		
321	✳	
815		
3752		
992		
991		
738		
402	○	
3776		
310	■	
975		

118

Happy Holidays

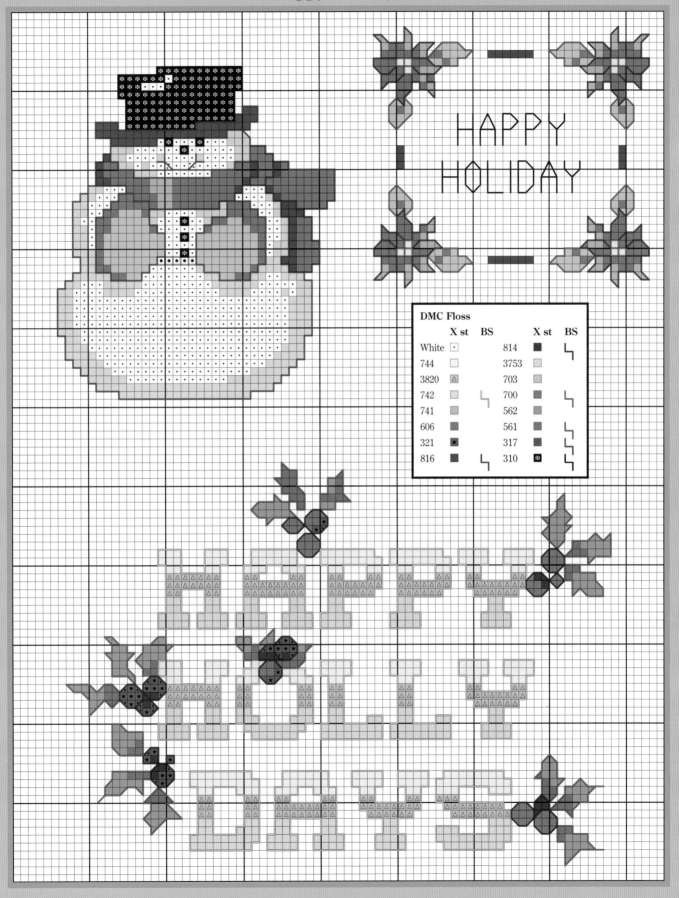

DMC Floss

	X st	BS		X st	BS
White	·		814	■	⌐
744			3753		
3820	▲		703		
742		⌐	700	■	⌐
741			562		
606	■		561	■	⌐
321	★		317	■	⌐
816	■	⌐	310	✳	⌐

HAPPY
HOLIDAY

Happy Holidays

Happy Holidays

DMC Floss

	X st	BS
White	·	
726		
741		
818		
606		
816		└
3753		
703		
700		└
317		└
310	❋	└

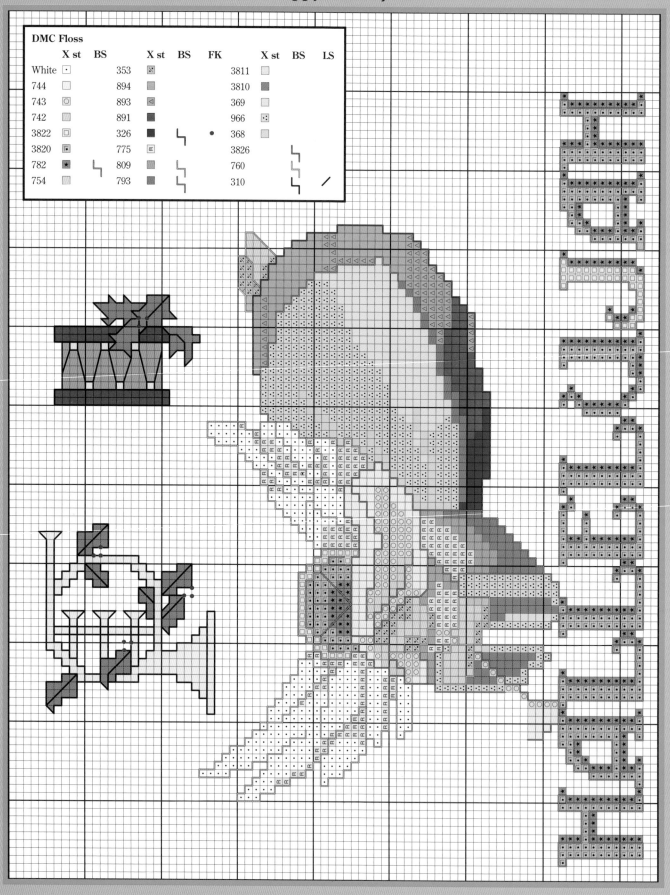

DMC Floss

	X st	BS		X st	BS
744			552		
742	+		800		
604			799		
602			3807		
666			3819		
498			704		
209			783		

Happy Holidays

DMC Floss							
	X st	BS		X st	BS		X st	BS
White	·		304	▨		911	▨	
945			902	▨	⌐	402		
783	▨	⌐	775	ℝ		318		⌐
776	⊞		3753			310	▨	⌐
603	▨		797	▨		921		⌐
601	▨		955			909		⌐
606	▨		913	♡		317		⌐
666	▨							

Happy Holidays

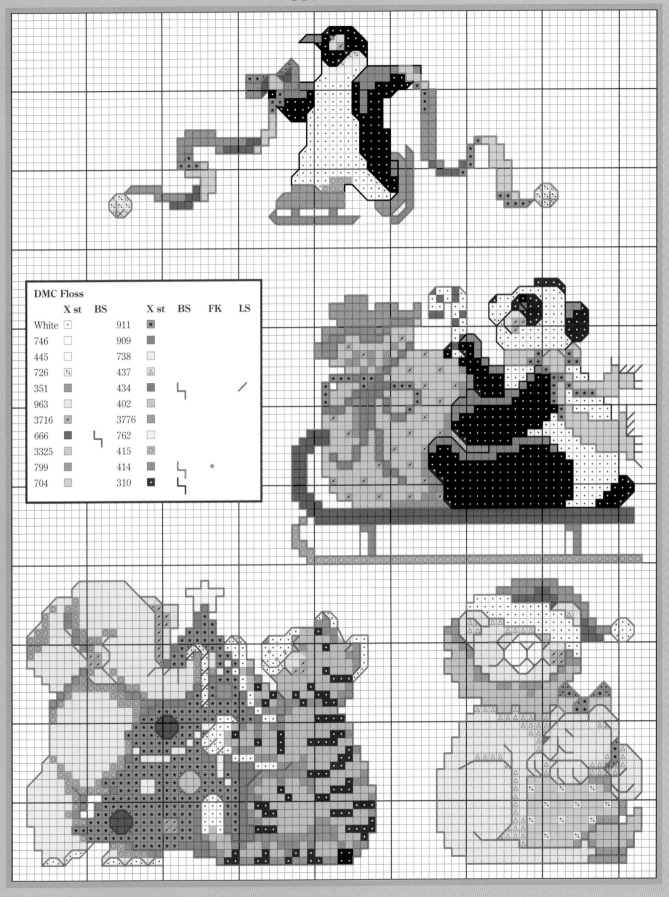

DMC Floss

	X st	BS		X st	BS	FK	LS
White	·		911	★			
746			909				
445			738				
726			437	△			
351			434		⌐		/
963			402				
3716			3776				
666		⌐	762				
3325			415	◎			
799			414		⌐	•	
704			310	■	⌐		

Happy Holidays

Happy Holidays

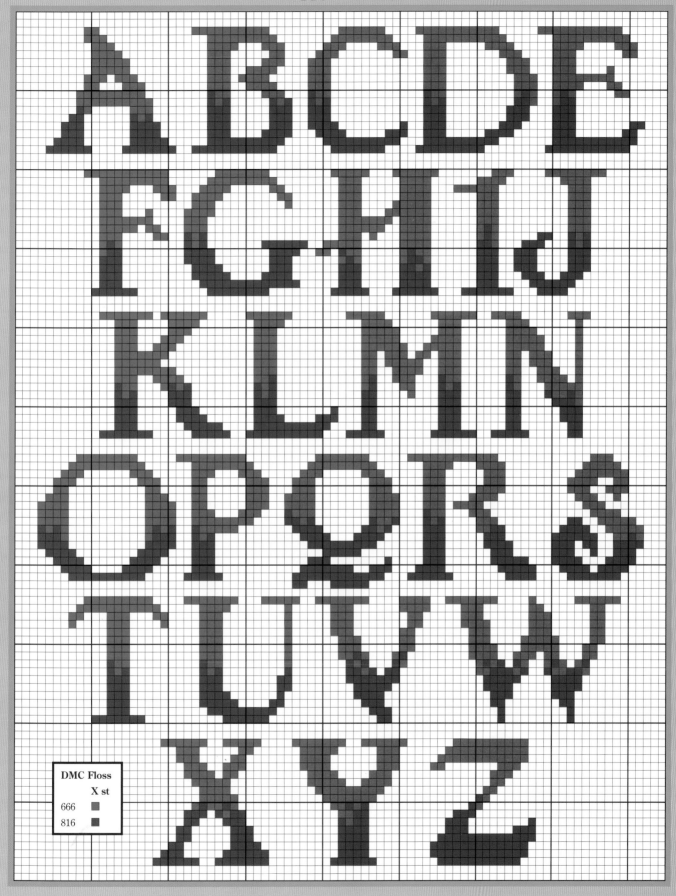

DMC Floss
X st

666 ▮
816 ▮

Metric Equivalency

MM-Millimetres CM-Centimetres

INCHES TO MILLIMETRES AND CENTIMETRES

INCHES	MM	CM	INCHES	CM	INCHES	CM
⅛	3	0.3	9	22.9	30	76.2
¼	6	0.6	10	25.4	31	78.7
½	13	1.3	12	30.5	33	83.8
⅝	16	1.6	13	33.0	34	86.4
¾	19	1.9	14	35.6	35	88.9
⅞	22	2.2	15	38.1	36	91.4
1	25	2.5	16	40.6	37	94.0
1¼	32	3.2	17	43.2	38	96.5
1½	38	3.8	18	45.7	39	99.1
1¾	44	4.4	19	48.3	40	101.6
2	51	5.1	20	50.8	41	104.1
2½	64	6.4	21	53.3	42	106.7
3	76	7.6	22	55.9	43	109.2
3½	89	8.9	23	58.4	44	111.8
4	102	10.2	24	61.0	45	114.3
4½	114	11.4	25	63.5	46	116.8
5	127	12.7	26	66.0	47	119.4
6	152	15.2	27	68.6	48	121.9
7	178	17.8	28	71.1	49	124.5
8	203	20.3	29	73.7	50	127.0

YARDS TO METRES

YARDS	METRES	YARDS	METRES	YARDS	METRES	YARDS	METRES	YARDS	METRES
⅛	0.11	2⅛	1.94	4⅛	3.77	6⅛	5.60	8⅛	7.43
¼	0.23	2¼	2.06	4¼	3.89	6¼	5.72	8¼	7.54
⅜	0.34	2⅜	2.17	4⅜	4.00	6⅜	5.83	8⅜	7.66
½	0.46	2½	2.29	4½	4.11	6½	5.94	8½	7.77
⅝	0.57	2⅝	2.40	4⅝	4.23	6⅝	6.06	8⅝	7.89
¾	0.69	2¾	2.51	4¾	4.34	6¾	6.17	8¾	8.00
⅞	0.80	2⅞	2.63	4⅞	4.46	6⅞	6.29	8⅞	8.12
1	0.91	3	2.74	5	4.57	7	6.40	9	8.23
1⅛	1.03	3⅛	2.86	5⅛	4.69	7⅛	6.52	9⅛	8.34
1¼	1.14	3¼	2.97	5¼	4.80	7¼	6.63	9¼	8.46
1⅜	1.26	3⅜	3.09	5⅜	4.91	7⅜	6.74	9⅜	8.57
1½	1.37	3½	3.20	5½	5.03	7½	6.86	9½	8.69
1⅝	1.49	3⅝	3.31	5⅝	5.14	7⅝	6.97	9⅝	8.80
1¾	1.60	3¾	3.43	5¾	5.26	7¾	7.09	9¾	8.92
1⅞	1.71	3⅞	3.54	5⅞	5.37	7⅞	7.20	9⅞	9.03
2	1.83	4	3.66	6	5.49	8	7.32	10	9.14

Index